George Patterson

The Heathen World

It's Need of the Gospel, And the Church's Obligation to Supply it

George Patterson

The Heathen World
It's Need of the Gospel, And the Church's Obligation to Supply it

ISBN/EAN: 9783744726092

Printed in Europe, USA, Canada, Australia, Japan

Cover: Foto ©Lupo / pixelio.de

More available books at **www.hansebooks.com**

THE HEATHEN WORLD;

ITS NEED OF THE GOSPEL,

AND

THE CHURCH'S OBLIGATION TO SUPPLY IT.

BY THE

REV. GEORGE PATTERSON, D.D.,

Author of "Memoir of Rev. James McGregor, D.D.," "The Doctrine of the Trinity Underlying the Revelation of Redemption," "Missionary Life Among the Cannibals," etc., etc.

"I am debtor both to the Greeks and to the Barbarians."
—Rom. i. 14.

TORONTO:
WILLIAM BRIGGS,
78 and 80 King Street East.

Montreal: C. W. Coates.   Halifax: S. F. Huestis.

1884.

PREFACE.

A FEW words seem to be necessary to explain the circumstances which have led to the publication of this essay. Deeply impressed with the condition of the heathen world—of its need of the Gospel, and of the obligation of the Church of Christ to supply that need—a gentleman offered a prize of a hundred guineas for the best essay on this important subject. The competition was open to the Dominion of Canada and Island of Newfoundland. The essays were required to be unsigned, bearing only some motto by which, *after* the prize had been awarded, the writer might be identified. Sealed envelopes containing the names of the writers, and having on the outside these distinguishing mottoes, were also to accompany the essays. The following-named gentlemen, representing different Churches, consented to act as adjudicators:—

    REV. WILLIAM CAVEN, D.D., *Principal of Knox College, Toronto;*

    REV. JOHN H. CASTLE, D.D., *President of Baptist Theological College, Toronto;*

Rev. Septimus Jones, M.A., *Professor of Apologetics, Wycliffe College (Church of England), Toronto;*

Rev. Henry D. Powis, *Pastor of Zion Congregational Church, Toronto;*

Rev. W. H. Withrow, D.D., *Editor of "Canadian Methodist Magazine," Toronto.*

The report of the adjudicators is given herewith.

It is the desire of the donor of the prize that, in the first place, it shall be sold at as low a price as possible, in order that by its wide circulation it may, in the greatest possible degree, quicken and intensify an interest in the all-important subject of the evangelization of the world; and, in the second place, that all profits accruing from the sales of the essay should be devoted to the object of promoting the interests of Christian missions in such way as the judgment of the adjudicators shall suggest.

REPORT OF ADJUDICATORS.

In response to the offer of a prize of one hundred guineas for the best essay on "The Heathen World: its need of the Gospel, and the Church's obligation to supply it," a large number of manuscripts were submitted in competition. Having carefully examined these, the adjudicators below-mentioned found that, while several of the essays exhibited a high degree of merit, the one bearing the motto, "I am debtor both to the Greeks and the barbarians," best fulfilled the conditions under which the competition was invited. To that essay, therefore, the prize was awarded. The envelope accompanying the MS. having been opened, the writer was discovered to be the Rev. GEORGE PATTERSON, D.D., Presbyterian minister at New Glasgow, N.S.

In view of the deep interest now being manifested throughout Protestant Christendom in the important work of the evangelization of the world, it is believed that this essay will prove a timely contribution to missionary literature. It is therefere sent forth with an earnest prayer that the end anticipated in offering the prize may be abundantly answered, and much good be accomplished by its widest possible circulation. We heartily recommend this volume to the friends of missions in all the Churches.

(Signed) WILLIAM CAVEN,
JOHN H. CASTLE,
SEPTIMUS JONES,
HENRY D. POWIS,
W. H. WITHROW.

CONTENTS.

	PAGE.
INTRODUCTION	xi

PART I.

THE HEATHEN WORLD.

CHAPTER I.

INDIA AND HINDOOISM	17
Section I.—Country and People	17
" II.—Early Hindooism	20
" III.—Caste	24
" IV.—Pantheism and Polytheism	28
" V.—Position of Woman under Hindooism	43

CHAPTER II.

LANDS OF THE BUDDHA AND THEIR RELIGION	48
Section I.—Countries and People	48
" II.—History and Principles of Buddhism	56
" III.—Practical Working of Buddhism	64

CHAPTER III.

SHAMANISM, AND THE DEVIL-WORSHIPPERS OF ASIA	75

CHAPTER IV.

CHINA, HER PEOPLE AND HER RELIGIONS	84
Section I.—Country and People	84
" II.—Their Religions	89

CHAPTER V.

RELIGIOUS OBSERVANCES AND MORAL CONDITION OF THE CHINESE	98
Section I.—Religious Observances	99
" II.—Moral Condition	112

CHAPTER VI.

	PAGE.
JAPAN AND HER RELIGIONS	120

CHAPTER VII.

AFRICA, HER PEOPLE AND HER RELIGIONS	127
Section I.—Country and People	127
" II.—The Bantu Tribes	129
" III.—The Negro Race	136
" IV.—Madagascar	150

CHAPTER VIII.

POLYNESIA	153
Section I.—Eastern Polynesia	153
" II.—Western Polynesia	158

CHAPTER IX.

THE HEATHEN IN AMERICA	172
CONCLUSION	184

PART II.

THE HEATHEN'S NEED OF THE GOSPEL.

Section I.—Idolatry a Heinous Sin before God	192
" II.—The Heathen Condemned	199
" III.—No Remedy but the Gospel	211

PART III.

THE DUTY OF THE CHURCH TO SUPPLY THE GOSPEL TO THE HEATHEN.

CHAPTER I.

THE GROUND OF MISSIONARY OBLIGATION THE COMMAND OF CHRIST	221
Section I.—The Command stated and illustrated	221
" II.—The Command enforced by the circumstances in which it was given	230

CHAPTER II.

THE COMMAND IN RELATION TO THE PREVIOUS DISPENSATIONS OF
GOD'S PROVIDENCE AND GRACE...................... 236

Section I.—The Command distinguishes the Old Testament
from the New 236
" II.—The Command the outcome of all God's purposes previously revealed.................. 243
" III.—God made preparation in Providence through centuries for carrying out the Command 252

CHAPTER III.

THE COMMAND ILLUSTRATED IN THE TEACHING OF OUR LORD... 253

CHAPTER IV.

THE COMMAND AS CARRIED INTO EXECUTION IN THE PRIMITIVE
CHURCH 260

Section I.—Preparation for it and commencement on the
day of Pentecost............:. 260
" II.—Steps by which the Church was led to engage fully in the work of evangelizing the Heathen 264
" III.—Prosecution of the work.................... 269

CHAPTER V.

PRESENT DUTY OF THE CHURCH TO THE HEATHEN 273

Section I.—Special claims of Missions to the Heathen..... 273
" II.—Duties of all Christians 281
" III.—Concluding appeal........................ 289

INTRODUCTION.

In surveying the "Faiths of the World," heathenism, while in its nature the most directly opposed to the character and claims of the Creator, will be seen at the same time to be the most extensive in its sway. More than one-half of our race are worshippers of idols. When we consider, in addition, how firmly the system is rooted in ancient custom and human corruption, it will be evident that in the great warfare which the Church of Christ is called to wage for the supremacy of Jehovah over the hearts and lives of men, this is her most formidable foe. The conflict with it is the one which will most seriously tax her resources, and which is likely to be the most prolonged.

To the successful prosecution of any war a first requisite is an accurate knowledge of the enemy. And in this great spiritual contest it is not less necessary that the Church should make herself thoroughly acquainted with the principles and working of all opposing systems, and particularly of this the greatest of all.

But while heathenism is one in its root principle of giving to some inferior object the honour that belongs to God alone, and alas! one also in its bitter fruits of sin and misery, yet in the course of ages it has assumed a great variety of forms. Men forsaking God and following their own inclinations or the guidance of Satan have chosen diverse objects for their worship, and served them by various modes of their own devising. Thus idolatry has assumed a great variety of forms, according to the mental character, history, social condition, or other circumstances of different races. Hence it becomes necessary, if we would fully appreciate the work before the Church, not only to know the general nature of heathenism, but to have some acquaintance with the distinctive features of the various systems of idol-worship now prevailing on the earth.

In considering, therefore, the claims of Christian missions to the heathen, our first duty in the following essay will be to contemplate "The Heathen World"—to view the countries and peoples still in Pagan darkness, and to sketch the particular forms of idolatry prevalent among them. In doing so it will not be in our power to trace, with any degree of minuteness, the formation and growth of any of these systems. All we can attempt is, to give a brief view of them as they are now found in actual operation in the life of the several races and tribes subject to them. If we refer to their past history, it will be only so far as it may seem necessary to illustrate this.

Such a review of the actual condition of the heathen will naturally lead to a consideration of their need of the Gospel as the Divine and only remedy for the evils under which they labour. Accordingly this will form the second subject of discussion. From this again we will be as naturally led to notice the duty of the Church to supply them with the means of life, forming the third and last topic to engage our attention.

PART I.
THE HEATHEN WORLD.

"Professing themselves to be wise, they became fools, and changed the glory of the incorruptible God for the likeness of an image of corruptible man, and of birds, and four-footed beasts, and creeping things."—Romans i. 22, 23.

THE HEATHEN WORLD.

CHAPTER I.

INDIA AND HINDOOISM.

"His spirit was provoked within him as he beheld the city FULL OF IDOLS."—Acts xvii. 16.

SECTION I.—COUNTRY AND PEOPLE.

IN proceeding to consider the heathen world as it now stands, India, from its past history, its extent and resources, the genius of its people, their numbers, their superstitions, so ancient, so strange, so evil, yet so firmly rooted in the minds of its votaries, and so fenced by philosophy, must claim our special attention. Our interest in this land is further deepened by the remarkable circumstances through which, in the providence of God, it has been brought under the control of Protestant England, and the prominent place which it has occupied in the modern missionary efforts of the Christian Church.

India forms a great triangle, jutting out from the continent of Asia, having for its base the Himalaya mountains, which rise to a height in some places of

29,000 feet, and stretch for a distance of 1,500 miles along its northern frontier. The principal part of the western coast is washed by the Arabian Sea, and the most of the eastern by the Bay of Bengal. Its length from north to south is over 1,900 miles, and its breadth from east to west, where it is widest, is nearly as great. It stretches from the 35th degree of North Latitude to the 8th, or from a temperate region through a great part of the torrid zone. Including British Burmah, which consists of the lower valley of the Irawadi and a long flat strip stretching along the east side of the Bay of Bengal, it contains an area of 1,485,952 square miles, divided as follows:—

Governed directly by Britain	880,098
Held by native rulers under British protection	604,590
Portuguese settlements	1,086
French settlements	178
	1,485,952

This is exclusive of the island of Ceylon, which contains an area of 25,742 square miles. India is thus equal to the whole of Europe, without Russia. It forms a continent rather than a single country, and presents every variety of scenery and climate, from the highest mountains in the world, with summits robed in perpetual snow, to river deltas, only a few inches above the level of the sea, and scorched with the most fiery tropical heat.

Its greatest riches are in its fertile soil, which yields almost every kind of vegetable production called for by the necessity or luxury of man, and that in such profusion, that in the great central plains, the husbandman reaps two and sometimes three crops a year. Indeed, the vegetation is so luxuriant as to be even dangerous, the rapid and excessive growth, with the equally rapid decay, producing the fevers and other diseases which are the great bane of the country. Its mineral wealth is also considerable.

By the census of 1881, the population amounted to over 254,000,000, equal to that of all Europe, without Russia, and more than double what Gibbon estimated the Roman Empire to contain in its palmiest days. Of these over 200,000,000, or about four-fifths reside in those Provinces directly under the British Government, and the remainder in those States under subordinate native rulers. Among them are spoken ninety-eight languages, with a much larger number of dialects.

In religion over fifty millions are Mohammedans,* and a million and three-quarters Christians, of whom the majority are Roman Catholics, leaving 200,000,000 of heathen. Of these, the Demon worshippers, Buddhists, Jains, and other adherents of systems different from the Brahmanical, may number twenty millions, leaving 180,000,000 votaries of Hindooism proper, which system we shall now attempt to describe.

---

* It is to be observed, however, that the large majority of the Mohammedans in India are half Hindoos. They observe the laws of caste, and practise many idolatrous ceremonies, so that by the standard of the Koran they would not be regarded as Moslems. But our present work is limited to the consideration of heathenism proper.

SECTION II.—EARLY HINDOOISM.

In order to obtain a distinct idea of the prevailing system of religion in India, commonly known as Brahmanism, it is necessary to refer to some of the chief events in the past history of the country.

The oldest books of the Hindoos are the hymns known as the Rig-Veda, some of which were in existence at least as early as B.C. 1200, or over 3,000 years ago. These poems exhibit the Hindoos as a branch of that great race which, from the name given to it in these productions, has in recent times been generally known as the Aryan, sometimes as the Indo-European, which originally had its home in the mountainous regions to the north of Hindostan. Thence various migrations had gone westward, forming the Celtic, Teutonic, Italic, and Greek branches of the family, and now another wave had flowed southward to India.

At the date of these hymns, this race had only advanced to the Punjaub and the banks of the Indus, while other races, known as Dasyas or natives, occupied the southern portions of the country. The former were fair in colour, but the latter are described as black. In the relation of these two, we have the origin of the system of caste, which forms so important a factor in the Hindoo social system. From the former sprang the Brahmans, Rajpoots, and other high castes, from the latter the hill tribes and low castes.

These poems show that at the time of their composition, the knowledge of the one living God among this people was obscured by nature worship. There is evidence to show that the race had originally worshipped one supreme, personal Deity. But they were now honouring other gods, whose names also expressed the phenomena of nature. The process by which they had come to this appears to have been, first, seeking to worship God in His works—looking through nature up to nature's God—and then transferring, as they soon did, this honour to the objects themselves. In such a state of thought, the object which is apt most strongly to strike the attention is the sky. Very generally it has been regarded as the divine abode; but at this time, under the name of Dyaus,* it was honoured as God. He was regarded as the husband of Prithini, the earth, from which together all things were produced. It is, however, in its nightly glory that it inspires the finest poetry of the primitive Hindoos. But with them this is no longer an appearance, but the god Varuna,† and the thousand stars are his thousand eyes spying the secrets of the earth. To him these poems address worship in strains so elevated that, if they were addressed to Him who dwells above the heavens, they might not offend the Christian sense. But in reality the authors had lost sight of the Creator, and their worship was directed to the creature.

Then, as the phenomena of nature were seen to be separate, men next came to honour them as distinct

---

* Same as Greek *Zeus*, or Latin Jupiter = *Zeus-pater*.
† Greek *ouranos*, Latin *uranus*.

gods. Thus these hymns render praise to Indra, the god of rain; Agni, the god of fire, manifested in the sun, the lightning, and fire; Vayu, the wind; Surya, the sun, etc. But instead of these gods having their respective spheres assigned them, as in the Greek mythology, there still lingered the idea of unity. The god that each worshipper addresses he addresses as supreme. It was only as in the lapse of time their conceptions became more gross, that they regarded their gods as having different interests, causing jealousies and quarrels. At this time the number of gods was reckoned at thirty-three.

At this time their worship consisted of such services as were deemed fitted to propitiate for sin—prostrations, chanting hymns, offerings of flowers and clarified butter; but chiefly sacrifices, as of cows, goats, horses, and men, the latter, as among all the ancient nations, being considered the most valuable. But all these services had reference, not to securing the divine favour in the future world, but to procuring present good, abundant crops, increase of children, long life, or success over enemies.

At this time none of those social customs which form the distinguishing features of the Hindooism of the present day, were to be found. There was nothing of caste as it now exists. There were the two races, the Aryan invaders and the aboriginal tribes; and there were differences of rank, but no inexorable law prevented an interchange of position, or bound the children of any class to one condition through all generations. There was none of the veneration for the cow, which may be regarded as the distinguishing peculiarity of Brahmanism, and her flesh was readily eaten. Polygamy was not legally recognized, and monogamy was the rule. Women, instead of being shut up in Zenanas, enjoyed a freedom of movement in public to which they have long been strangers. They were not in childhood disposed of in marriage at the will of their guardians, but allowed freedom of choice when of suitable age. The cruel rite of Suttee had no existence, and the re-marriage of widows, the forbidding of which has been such a fruitful source of misery and degradation, was freely admitted.

The various native tribes had their worship, at that time very distinct from that of the Aryan race, probably fetichism and demon worship among the lowest, and tree and serpent worship among the more advanced. The intermixture of their rites with those of the conquering race, has been an important element in the formation of the Hindooism of the present day. We should here observe that these native tribes, to a large extent, yet preserve a marked distinction from the conquering race in appearance, language, and even religion.

These old hymns are still professedly held in honour by the Hindoos of the present day, but in reality modern Hindooism is noted by its contrast with their teaching. There is an immense mass of literature of later date, more or less of a sacred character. But the real religious books of India are the Puranas, supposed to have been compiled between the 8th and 16th centuries. These, while containing many excellent moral precepts, are such a mass of contradictions, exaggerations, absurdities, and indecencies, that the missionaries draw from them their most telling arguments against the system.*

SECTION III.—CASTE.

We begin with this because it is in reality not only the most characteristic feature of Hindooism, but because it is a foundation principle of the system. A man may worship any God he pleases, and in the way he thinks best, yet if he adheres to the laws of caste, he retains his position as a good Hindoo; but if he violates one of its rules, he is regarded as an outcast for this life and the next.

Caste, as we have said, originated in the conquest of the country by the Aryan race, the higher castes being the representatives of the conquerors, and the lower of the conquered. But this can give very little idea of what the system has become. About 600 years after the date assigned for the Rig-Veda, and about as long before the birth of Christ, it appears fully developed. In the writings of that period, we find mention of the four castes—the Brahmans, or the praying ones, next to them the Kshatryas or warriors, below them again the Vaisyas, or merchants and agri-

---

* But even portions of the Rig-Veda, from their indecency, cannot be translated into English.

culturists, while beneath all were the Sudras or labourers.

The first three classes were known as twice born, the last as only once. Already the distinction between them was regarded as founded on their original creation, the first having proceeded from the mouth of Brahm, the second from his arm, the third from his thigh, and the last from his foot. The distinction between them has ever since been believed to be quite as decided as between different races of animals.

The same divisions are still recognized, but the second and third classes have nearly disappeared, leaving only the Brahmans and Sudras, but these are divided into a large number of what we may call sub-castes. The number of these in Travancore is eighty-two, and in some other provinces they are much more numerous.

These castes are not generally allowed to intermarry, though in some cases a Brahman may marry a low-caste woman, the children following the caste of the mother. They are not allowed to eat or drink together, or even to draw water out of the same well. A high-caste man must not eat food that has been cooked or even touched by one of low caste. Even the shadow of a low-caste man passing over food cooking, would render it polluted for a man belonging to a higher caste. They cannot worship in the same buildings, and in some instances a low-caste man is not allowed to touch the outermost wall of a Brahman temple. In any case, he is not allowed to read the sacred books.

The position of the high-caste man is supposed to be the result of meritorious works in a previous state of existence, and that of the low-caste man the consequence of his former misdeeds. For this reason, as well as from the birth of the Brahmans from the mouth of Brahm, they are treated with extravagant honours, indeed may be said to be worshipped as gods. In native states, there are fixed distances, beyond which members of lower castes dare not approach them. Europeans have been forbidden to use the main roads, lest too great nearness to a Brahman might defile him, and missionaries have been assaulted and beaten who refused to remove from the highway when one of this class was passing; while under native law Brahmans are exempt from capital punishment, whatever be their crime.

On the principles of this system, the Brahmans hold that were one of them to quit his proper work, were he for example to make his living by manual labour, rather than by teaching or begging, but especially were he to lose caste, by violating any of its laws regarding association with other castes, he would, to expiate his offence, have his birth in the next state in some miserable condition, as that of a vomit-eating demon. On the other hand, they teach that a Sudra by fulfilling the duties of his station here, will gain an advance of position in his next birth. The duties which they specially insist on, are serving the Brahmans, worshipping and feeding them as present deities. The neglect of these obligations, they hold, will insure the most wretched form of existence in the life to come. The lower castes enter into these views, and are often as great sticklers for the system as the higher.

These facts, however, will only give a faint idea of the working of the system. As the Sanscrit professor at Oxford says: "It is difficult for Europeans to understand how the pride of caste, as a divine ordinance, inter-penetrates the whole being of a Hindoo. He looks upon his caste as his veritable god; and those caste rules, which we believe to be a hindrance to his adoption of the true religion, are to him the very essence of all religion, for they influence his whole life and conduct."

We cannot stay to point out the widespread evils of caste, but must notice its effects upon morality. It lays its whole stress on ceremonial, rather than moral, purity. A Brahman may commit theft, adultery or murder, and not lose caste here, or suffer any loss hereafter; but any violation of caste rules, eating cows' flesh, becoming a Christian, a high-caste man eating food prepared by one of a low caste, or a Sudra insulting a Brahman, will involve the guilty in degradation, through many myriad forms of repulsive life. The result of such teaching cannot be doubtful, while the inveteracy of its hold upon the minds of all classes, has surprised even those best acquainted with Hindoo character.

The common bond of union among all these castes is reverence for the cow. They do not regard it as a god, or pray to it to receive blessings, but whatever be the god they worship, they look upon the cow as a sacred animal, by means of which caste is preserved or restored when lost. Hence, to kill a cow is a worse crime than murder, and to die with a cow's tail in the hand is to secure an immediate passage to bliss.

SECTION IV.—PANTHEISM AND POLYTHEISM.

To the observer of Hindooism, the aspect which it first presents is that of an incongruous and degrading polytheism. Instead of the thirty-three gods of the Rig-Veda, he hears now of three hundred and thirty millions; and even on a glimpse at its rites, he is amazed at their absurdity or shocked by their vileness. Macaulay, in a well-known passage, thus describes the system: "In no part of the world has a religion ever existed more unfavourable to the moral and intellectual health of the race. The Brahmanical mythology is so absurd that it necessarily debases every mind which receives it as truth. And with this absurd mythology is bound up an absurd system of physics, an absurd geography, an absurd astronomy. Nor is this form of paganism more favourable to art than to religion. Through the whole of the Hindoo Pantheon you will look in vain for anything resembling the majestic forms which stood in the shrines of ancient Greece. All is hideous and grotesque and ignoble. As this superstition is of all superstitions the most irrational, and of all superstitions the most inelegant, so is it of all superstitions the most immoral. Emblems of vice are objects of public worship. The courtezans are as much a part of the establishment of the temple, as much the ministers of the god, as the priests. Crimes against life, crimes against property, are not only permitted, but enjoined by this odious theology. But for our interference, human victims would still be offered to the Ganges, the widow would still be laid on the pile by the corpse of her husband, and be burned alive by her own children. It is by the command and under the protection of one of the most powerful goddesses that the Thugs join themselves to the unsuspecting traveller, make friends with him, slip the noose round his neck, plunge their knives into his eyes, hide him in the earth, and divide his money and baggage."

Such is one view of the heathenism of India, but he who penetrates no deeper than this has little idea of the system, or of the manner in which it is entrenched behind exceedingly subtle philosophical speculations. Let him converse with an educated Hindoo, and he will find him speaking of God as *One*, and quoting their sacred books as teaching that truth, at the very time that he recognizes the gods many of this system. Even the common people, in their ordinary conversation, speak of God as one. Closer intercourse will reveal a mode of thinking among them strange to most Western minds. It will show that this people, possessing perhaps the most acute intellects found among men, have elaborated a scheme or schemes of Pantheistic philosophy, which have led scholars in the West to declare that in the regions of pure thought they have distanced Western thinkers. It will reveal that not only will the learned pundit openly propound the principles of Pantheism, but that the ordinary peasant has in his own way grasped and is able to apply them. It is because the body, so faithfully depicted by Macaulay, is animated by this subtle soul, that Hindooism is the power it is found to be, perhaps the greatest with which Christianity has to contend in these latter days.

Difficult as it is to convey, in the space at our disposal, an idea of the philosophy by which Hindoo idolatry is maintained, it is necessary to attempt it, if we would give anything like a correct view of the Brahmanical system. *

The great central point of difference between Christianity and Hindooism lies just in this, that while the latter acknowledges a great Unity, the one Supreme Spirit, *it is not a personal God.* We have seen how the early Hindoos, after they had come to regard the separate entities of the universe as distinct divinities, still retained the idea of unity in the Supreme. It was not a great stretch therefore from that point, to lose the finite in the infinite, to regard all existence as parts of one whole, and to merge all in the one all-pervading, all-comprising Being. At all events, the Hindoo Pantheist, setting out with the principle that

---

* In the following account of the Pantheism of the Hindoos, I have closely followed Robson in his work, "Hindooism in Relation to Christianity." To it I am also indebted for part of the information contained in another section of this chapter.

out of nothing nothing can be made, not only maintains man's previous existence, but goes farther, and argues that there is only one existent spirit—that the human spirit emanated from it, and must return to it. Man and God are one, Hindoos generally will say, and the great object of man should be to attain to this final absorption in the Supreme.

If the objection be raised, that so far from our consciousness indicating any connexion between us and the Supreme, it on the contrary shows limitations and imperfections, which are contradictory to the idea of God, the Hindoo replies that this is owing to delusion or *Maya*. The visible universe is but a projection of the Supreme, as the shadow is of a pillar. This enveloping us gives us the impression of our individual existence, and at the same time of a world around us, which we believe to be external to ourselves. This however is only as in a dream the scenes seem real, but on our awakening are seen to be illusion.

Not man alone, but everything material, as well as immaterial, they regard as an outgoing of the great self-existent. Spirit is imprisoned in animals, trees and stones. This is one with the Supreme Spirit, and its final end is, being freed from all limitations, to be identified with it.

But will not man be free to join it at death? Here the doctrine of transmigration of souls intervenes. To this probably they had been led, as an explanation of the mysteries of Providence, regarding the distribution of good and evil. But according to it, men's spirits are bound by chains both of the good and evil deeds, done in former states, requiring them to pass through various births, finding no rest until they are at last delivered from the idea of their own personality. This is the Liberation to which they look forward as the final object of desire.

These ideas they illustrate by a comparison of the ocean. The water in it is one, so is the great Spirit. But as a portion of the ocean is exhaled in vapour, so a portion of the great spirit is exhaled in connection with or in the form of matter, or under illusion. The water ascending in vapour, assumes the form of clouds, is driven by the winds, descends in rain, forms the streams, and flows to the ocean, so when any portion of the great spirit is thus exhaled, it must pass through men and animals, gods and devils, trees and rivers, and even stones, forced by the deeds committed either in that or some previous birth, to enter into another, until it has passed the full number of eighty-four hundred thousand. Then its good and evil deeds having received their due reward, it will be emancipated and join the Supreme.

In this view, it becomes the great aim to shorten the process, and reach the issue by some quicker route. This is called "cutting off the eighty-four." But how is this to be attained. Philosophic Hindooism replies, that it is not by works, but by getting quit of all works. The way of knowledge is the way of salvation, and meditation the means by which that is to be gained. To retire from the world, and, avoiding works, to concentrate contemplation upon self, seeking to realize its identity with the all-spirit around, until one is persuaded that he is god, is the way to obtain Liberation.

But, of course, all cannot follow the life of a recluse, though this is the highest and the most certain way to the end. Besides, to admit all to follow that course, would be to raise other castes to the level of the Brahman. Hence the multitude have been left to follow their own way. In fact, the various tribes never gave up their old idols, nor were they likely to do so for Pantheism. Practically it is about on a level with atheism. The All-god as little meets the wants of the human heart as No-god. Instead, therefore, of attempting to supplant the old systems of worship, Brahmanism entered into alliances with them, allowing each tribe to retain its own god or gods, and to worship in its own way. It even admitted that that way led its votaries, though more slowly, toward the same issue that the recluse gained by meditation. They had only to acknowledge the divinity of the holy Brahmans and reverence the cow, to become incorporated into the Hindoo system; and they were not only permitted, but taught that it was their duty, to follow still their old worship, being bound to it by their previous birth. Thus was formed the Hindooism of these later days, and the comparatively pure worship of the old Aryan race, became the incongruous polytheism which India now presents.

But the question still remains, How is their polytheistic worship reconciled with the Pantheistic philosophy, which we have endeavoured to describe? The view of the Hindoo is, that we are so far removed from the great Supreme as to be unable of ourselves to reach to unity with it, but that the gods have more power to promote the object than men, and farther that they are influenced by motives, and can be brought under the power of the worshipper. In all Vedic worship, there is the idea that the religious services exercise an influence to which these beings must succumb. Men by the intensity of their devotion may compel the gods to look upon them with favour, and help them forward in their progress. Indeed, by his worship, the Hindoo supposes that he becomes united to his god, and is thus carried forward to the ultimate goal, to be absorbed in Brahm. The result is, that while Pantheism is so diffused among all classes in India, that the peasant regards his inner self as Deity, there is no country that so well answers the apostle's description, as being "full of idols." The state of matters in this respect is thus described by a recent writer:

"There is a strange mixture of aboriginal Fetichism with Brahmanical Pantheism in the popular religion of the mass of the people. Everything great and useful, everything strange, monstrous and unusual, whether good or evil, is held to be permeated by the presence of divinity. It is not merely all the mighty phenomena and forces of the universe—all the most striking manifestations of almighty power—that excite the awe and attract the reverence of the ordinary Hindoo. There is not an object on earth or in heaven which he is not prepared to worship—rocks, stocks and stones, trees, pools and rivers, his own implements of trade, the animals he finds most useful, the noxious reptiles he fears; men remarkable for any extraordinary qualities—for great valour, sanctity, virtue, or even vice; good and evil demons, ghosts and goblins, the spirits of departed ancestors, an infinite number of semi-human semi-divine existences—inhabitants of the seven upper and the seven lower worlds—each and all of these come in for a share of divine honour, or a tribute of more or less adoration. Verily, the Hindoo Pantheon has a place for everybody and everything. The principal deities are merely the occupants of its most conspicuous niches. To attempt an exhaustive enumeration of its minor gods and goddesses would be a hopeless task; and to count the ever-multiplying army of its martyrs, saints and sages would be a simple impossibility. New shrines are continually springing up, to receive the remains of holy men or ascetics—examples of extraordinary sanctity, or some peculiar manifestation of the divine energy, who after death are canonized and deified."*

We have already mentioned that Hindooism professes to have three hundred and thirty millions of gods; but in fact only about sixty are worshipped to any extent. The three principal are Brahma, Vishnu and Siva. The great supreme, uniting himself with

---

* "Hindooism," by Professor Monier Williams.

energy, produced or became these three, the first of whom is named the creator, or re-former, for matter is regarded as eternal; the second the preserver; and the last the destroyer. In the same way were produced three female forms—Shoroshoti, Luksmi and Bhogoboti, or Parvoti, the same as Dourga, who became the consorts of the first three respectively. Of the other gods, Gunnesh, or Gaupati, is the favourite in Southern India. He is represented in the form of a short, fat man, with an elephant's head, four hands, and sitting on a rat. He is a glutton and a debauchee, but the patron of literature. Then there is another form of Krishna, Jagannath, "the Lord of the world," who had his shrine at Orissa, to which hundreds of thousands go on pilgrimages from distances of hundreds of miles, of whom thousands die unpitied and unaided by the wayside. He is represented as an old stump of an idol, the legs of which have rotted off, owing to his immorality.

No country is so distinguished by the number of its temples, shrines and symbols of idolatry as India. The smallest village will have its idols of wood or stone, set in every prominent place, as on the summit of the hills or under stately trees. Then there are hundreds of sacred places, cities, confluences of rivers, tanks, monasteries, spots consecrated by the presence or deeds of the most noted male or female divinities, the very soil of which is supposed to exhale sanctity for the present life, and bliss for the future. The most revered of these is Benares, the whole soil of which, with the country round within a radius of ten miles, is supposed to be a part of heaven, let down to earth. So sacred is it deemed that any person dying there, even an unclean European, goes to some heaven. It has two thousand temples, with shrines and idols numbered by the hundred thousand, and twenty-five thousand resident Brahmans. Devout Hindoos seek to visit it once in their lives, and many go there to die. Take a glance at the scenes here presented, as seen by Mr. Bainbridge, in "the golden temple"— "The revolting picture is the same we have witnessed at scores of places all over India. The sacred cows are strolling around the enclosures. A woman seizes the tail of one, and with the holy excrements bathes her face. Obscene idols are all around. The Linga surrounded by the Yoni are the most conspicuous objects of worship. Siva, and Parvoti or Dourga, are being propitiated by multitudes with libations and garlands. It is all unspeakably vile, and self-respect compels retreat." Almost equally sacred is the Ganges throughout all its length. It can remove the greatest sins; and to die on its banks is the surest passport to bliss.

But the main divisions of Hindoo worship are two —those which have as their respective objects Vishnu and Siva, Brahma being little regarded, as he is considered as having accomplished his work. Their votaries are known as Vaishnavas and Saivas, and are distinguished by the former having a frontal mark of three perpendicular lines, and that of the latter being three horizontal ones. Their modes of worship are entitled, "The way of devotion" and "The way of works;" and they form two sects, which were long in violent antagonism.

Vishnu is represented as black or blue, having four arms, and riding on a creature half man and half bird. His symbol is the serpent, and hence the sacredness attached to that animal. He is supposed to have become incarnate nine times, sometimes in the form of animals, as the boar, the tortoise, and the fish. But his eighth incarnation was as Krishna, a former hero of Hindoo history. Many tales of him are current, which represent him as characterized in boyhood by thievery, and in manhood by unmentionable crimes. Yet this incarnation, which represents their god as revelling in boundless licentiousness, is the favourite with millions. His images are more common than any other, and they are designed to represent his performances. "It is a shame," says one writer, "even to speak of the things which Krishna unblushingly practised. Yet Hindoos of both sexes recount the foul narrative, not only without shame, but with positive fervour and devotion." The learned try to allegorize these tales, but the common people gloat over them in all their foulness. They do not deny that if a man were to commit such deeds, he would be the object of reprobation, but for a god to do so, only shows his greater power and liberty.

Siva is known by such names as "the furious," "lord of devils," etc. He is generally regarded as having been a mendicant, who gained his power by austerities, but at the same time legend pictures him as one delighting in revelry, smoking intoxicating drugs, cruelty and slaughter, as well as licentiousness, though, as Robson says, "his vice differs from that of Krishna, very much as a half-idiotic boor's might differ from that of a prince." He is represented as having a third eye in his forehead, a glance from which is supposed to strike dead all who offend him, and as wearing a rosary and necklace of human skulls, while serpents entwine round his neck.

We may observe, that in all heathen worship there is nothing of what we associate with the idea, as adoration, prayer and seeking spiritual good. In the worship of both Vishnu and Siva, they are invoked as the supreme spirit, as Ram or Rama. The wise say that this is merely as an aid to memory, but the mass suppose that there is virtue in the mere repetition of the name, even without intelligence or design on the part of the worshipper, and that the god is thus put under obligations, as a merchant who receives money.

But more commonly they are worshipped through images. Some may take a philosophic view of the subject, and regard these as symbols, and as such, aids to devotion. Others consider that by the Brahman's charms, the image becomes the shrine of the Deity, while a third class, probably the majority, believe that by the same process it has been made a god, and able of its own power and will to benefit its votaries.

The doctrine of the Vaishnavas is, that what is

required in worship is *Bhakti*, or simple faith in their god. This they manifest by certain expressions of respect, which they accompany with offerings, intended as food for him. Thus he is pleased, and will help them on their way to Liberation. One who has been guilty of such crimes as Krishna, is expected not to be severe upon the conduct of his votaries, and accordingly many act upon this principle, so that this worship is called the self-indulgent way of salvation. Within their temples are enacted scenes of which it is a shame even to speak.

Of Siva worship again, the main principle is, that power over the gods is obtained by austerities, and hence it is called the way of works. But its works are simply self-torture, and the greater the pain the higher the merit. Hence such practices as lying on a bed of spikes, holding up the arm till it is withered, keeping silence for twelve years, being scorched by five fires, gazing on the mid-day sun till the organ of vision is destroyed, are regarded as acts so meritorious, as to hasten the ultimate end—absorption into the supreme. In these things there is no idea of subduing any passion. The missionary, who has conversed with such ascetics, has found beneath all these austerities the exhibition of a sordid, selfish, soul. As their god, too, with all his austerity, was not free from sensuality, multitudes of his disciples follow his example. There are secret communities who connect with their worship rites of the most revolting and sensual character. This is particularly the case with the *Shaktas*, the worshippers of *Shakti*, the female principle. They have also religious books called *Tantras*, which teach a religion of works, but the works are violations of sobriety, decency and truth.

"Parvoti, the wife of Siva, is represented by goddesses of immense popularity at the present day. In Bengal, Dourga and Kali may be said to monopolize the devotion of the masses. The latter of these has her principal shrine in the city of Calcutta, which derives its name from her. No object more frightful than Kali could well be looked upon; her character is as dark as her name and her person—(*Kali*, black). Her delight is in blood; under her protection and blessing the Thugs of India carried out their diabolical system of treachery and murder; human blood is to her most grateful of all; in former days children used to be slaughtered before her shrine; at the present time she has to content herself with the blood of animals alone. Repeatedly have we in passing her temple seen the sacrificial stream flowing; as many as 200 animals, chiefly goats, are sometimes slain there in one day."* In this the votaries will roll themselves, before prostrating themselves before the hideous statue, with its protruding tongue red with freshly applied blood, its necklace of infant skulls, and its hands holding a knife, a bleeding heart, and a skull.

We cannot dwell farther on Hindoo worship, and, from what has been said, it will not be necessary to

---

* Vaughan's "The Trident, the Crescent, and the Cross."

add much on the subject of their morality. In regard to this we must not indulge in indiscriminate abuse. Harm has been done here by exaggeration. It should be acknowledged that many of this people are exemplary in the discharge of relative duties. Millions of wives are faithful and affectionate, multitudes of men are kind and hospitable; as a race they are gentle and of temperate habits, so that Bishop Heber said, that with all their faults, he "would think it impossible to live among them without loving them." They "show the work of the law written on their hearts." But if there is any virtue among them, it is in spite of their religion. It is only necessary to advert to three points, which have been brought out in this discussion, to show how it tends to subvert all morality. First, their Pantheism uproots its very foundation. According to this system, evil as well as good is a manifestation of the Supreme Spirit. Hence a Hindoo will deny the criminality of the worst acts, theft, lewdness, or murder, at least on his part, as, according to his creed, they are the acts of God. Secondly, Their gods are represented as guilty of the foulest crimes, and the favourite ones are monsters of vice. "They that make them are like unto them." The low moral condition, which could fashion such gods, must in turn be farther deteriorated by the worship of them. And, thirdly, much of the very worship in their temples are acts of unmentionable foulness. The tendency of this we need not stay to describe.

SECTION V.—POSITION OF WOMAN UNDER HINDOOISM.

The degradation of woman marks all systems of heathenism; but as her treatment among the Hindoos is closely connected with their religion, it is necessary to refer to it particularly. According to the code of Manu, women have no minds, and the Brahmans teach that their present condition, like that of the maimed and the diseased, is the result of sin in some previous state of existence. It will thus be seen, that all the wrongs inflicted on the female sex in India, if they did not originate in the Hindoo religion, are now, at all events, grounded upon it.

With people holding such a view, we are the less surprised that the birth of a daughter should be received, even by the mother, with bitter lamentations, the house in which such an event has taken place being, as they say, "accursed," and that the unwelcome stranger should meet with ill treatment or run the risk of infanticide. Formerly infants, both boys and girls, were thrown by devotee mothers into the Ganges, as an offering to the goddess Gunga, to secure their salvation. But apart from this religious rite, thousands perished simply because they were girls. So dreadful did the evil become, that the British Government stepped in to stop it, and the offering of infants to the Ganges no longer takes place. But infanticide still prevails in secret, particularly among the Rajpoot high castes, who dread the possibility of their daughters being connected with castes below them. A government officer found in one village only eight girls under twelve to eighty boys.

The code of Manu also says: "The husband gives bliss to his wife here below, and *he will give her happiness in the next world.*" Hence it also lays down the following regulation: "Every man shall give his daughter in marriage to an excellent and handsome youth of the same caste, even *though she has not attained the age of eight years.*" With this idea, if spared in infancy, girls in India are invariably married or betrothed when mere children, it may be to some old or middle-aged man, to add to the number of his female slaves, or to some boy scarcely older than herself, and this at the will or according to the convenience of her relatives; and though in the latter case she may scarcely have seen her betrothed, yet if he die she will endure all the evils of widowhood.

From the time of her betrothal she is no longer legally under the control of her parents, but is entirely at the disposal of her husband and his mother, though the actual marriage may not take place then. If they are poor she becomes the slave and household drudge of the latter. If more wealthy, she is shut up in the Zenana.* While her husband's apartments may be furnished in style and comfort, hers are the worst, the

---

* It may be proper to explain that this word means "place of the women," and denotes the apartments in the establishment of the wealthy reserved for the female members of the family. The word is not used in every part of India, but the other words employed express the same idea.

darkest, and the least ventilated in the establishment. Here she is kept from all intercourse with the world, and shut out from every source of knowledge. Her existence is so completely ignored that she is never spoken of before a stranger; and were one to enquire for her it would be resented as a serious affront. No man eats with his wife; and to converse familiarly or on equal terms with her would subject him to great loss of respect. While of the whole population of India scarcely six per cent. can read and write, not one in two hundred females possesses these accomplishments; and so ignorant are they that a Zenana worker tells of the wife of a wealthy man who had not only never seen a river, but could not form a conception of running water. Here life at best is burdensome from *ennui*. "To dress her hair, count her jewels and costly robes, play with trinkets, dolls and toys of childhood, amuse herself with gossip about other Zenanas, play with her children, or teach them to bow down to idols —these things sum up her existence."

But often she is treated with cruelty, for which there is no more relief than for the inmates of the dungeons of the Inquisition, and from which many take refuge in suicide. In particular, at the time of her greatest need and sharpest agony, she is thrust out as unclean into a dark, dirty shed in the courtyard, with a mud floor, there to pass her first few weeks of motherhood. By this cruelty many lives are lost, and many constitutions permanently weakened. In such cases her only hope and consolation rests in the birth of a son, for then the father will honour her for his sake, and if she dies she will have a son to light her funeral pyre, by which her soul will go straight to heaven.

Then there is polygamy, with its quarrels, jealousies and other evils. Many, from poverty, have only one wife; but the more a man takes the more servants he has. The practice is greatly encouraged by the Brahmanical tenet, to which we have referred, that only through her husband can a woman gain heaven. Hence Mr. Ward mentions that fathers will make any sacrifices to marry their daughters to Brahmans, and that some of the latter will be maintained in this way, marrying scores of women, professing thus to confer upon them eternal salvation, and thereafter going from house to house receiving support from their families.

The code of Manu taught the duty of women to sacrifice themselves for their husbands; but his precepts clearly show that this was to be done while living. Brahmanism, in its development as a religious system, first recommended, then commanded, their immolation. This is the well-known rite of Suttee, which long had such a hold upon the Hindoo mind, and which was only abolished by the strong arm of British authority in 1830.

A missionary at Calcutta, writing a short time before, says that within a few miles of his house more than a hundred widows were immolated every year, and that the number sacrificed in the whole Province of Bengal in the same period was 570. Many of these were mere children, and their boy-husbands they might have seldom seen. Between 1815 and 1820 there came under the notice of government the cases of sixty-two girls under eighteen thus destroyed. Of these, ten were only twelve years of age, one was ten, and three were only eight; and a case is mentioned where, on the death of a man of rank, the number of his wives sacrificed was twenty-five. Though this rite has been suppressed by government, yet only this power prevents its being still practised by zealous Hindoos. In place of it, widows are doomed to a social martyrdom; and such is the degradation of their condition, such the contempt and cruelty with which they are treated, that some seek relief in suicide.

Such is the condition of ninety millions of our fellow-beings, while that of twenty-one millions of Mohammedans in India is little better. Indeed, it seems indubitable that the seclusion and much of the treatment which women receive in that country, are the direct result of the rule of the latter. At all events, as has been justly said, "in no country, nor indeed in any age, have an equal number of human beings been more helpless, more ignominiously treated, or liable to equal suffering."*

---

* "India," An Outline Missionary Series, published by Snow & Co.

CHAPTER II.

LANDS OF THE BUDDHA AND THEIR RELIGION.

"The fool hath said in his heart, There is no God. They are corrupt, they have done abominable works."—Psalms xiv. 1.

SECTION I.—COUNTRIES AND PEOPLE.

THE whole of Northern, Central and Eastern Asia is occupied, with very slight exceptions, by different races of that great division of the human family now commonly known as the Mongolian. These differ considerably in appearance; many of the nomad tribes in the interior having abundance of animal food, as well as the milk, butter and cheese of their flocks and herds, enjoying plenty of fresh air, and living a free and active life, are strong, able-bodied, well-made men; while those in the marshy rice-fields or the heated jungles of the South-Eastern coast are below the middle size, and ungainly in appearance. There is found among them every variety of social life—the agricultural industry of the Chinese, the manufacturing skill of the Japanese, the bold seamanship of the Malay, with the nomad habits of the Tartar huntsmen, shepherds and herdsmen of the interior, and the barbarism of the Turki tribes, which have been pronounced the least civilized of human beings. Still they have so much in common physically, that they are regarded as a variety of the human family, almost as marked as the negro. They are described as having yellow-brown skins, black eyes and hair, flat noses, oblique eyes, and little hair on the body or face.

With the exception of Turkestan, including Bokhara and Khiva on the West, of which the inhabitants are Mohammedans, and Siberia on the North, where they retain their old heathenism, the whole of the regions which we have described as inhabited by the Mongols may be considered as either wholly or partially under the influence of the system of religion known as Buddhism. Indeed, it is held that the teaching of Buddha, the founder of the system, rules the minds of a larger number of the human race than any other religious creed. If we include China and Japan, this is undoubtedly true. In this way the adherents of the system have been reckoned at over 500,000,000. But these two countries are only partially Buddhist, both of them having their own religions, as well as their own civilizations; and even where they have adopted Buddhism, it has been with modifications. Reserving these for separate consideration, and deducting for China 300,000,000 and for Japan 34,000,000, there will still remain a large number of adherents of this system, scattered over immense regions of country, at which we can barely glance.

First, we should mention that the island of Ceylon, though of India geographically, is mainly a Buddhist country. Of its population of 2,406,262 souls, 1,520,575 are Buddhists, and only 465,944 Hindoos. Buddhism was introduced about 300 B.C., and now exists there in its pristine purity. Then to the East of India lies the Indo-Chinese peninsula, embracing Burmah, Siam and Cochin China. The first embraces British Burmah, extending along the Eastern shore of the Bay of Bengal, with a population of 2,747,148, of whom 2,447,831 are Buddhists, and Independent Burmah, still having a territory of 190,000 square miles, or as large as France. By its present boundary, it has no maritime territory, and no large alluvial tracts. It is generally an upland country, rich in mineral resources, with mountains yielding the finest timber. Though not equally fertile with the low-lying parts of British Burmah, yet it produces abundantly fruit, grain, rice, and the richest pasturage. The population is estimated at 4,000,000, the majority Buddhists.

"The present government of Independent Burmah," says Bainbridge, "is the worst in the world, with the possible exception of Dahomey and Ashanti. It is a despotism of the most stern, cruel and unmitigated character. All the property of the realm and all the lives of the people belong to the savage upon the throne. Recently, in 'the light of Asia,' he massacred all his relatives, to the number of three hundred, all who could by the most remote possibility interfere with his brutal sovereignty. And the history of Burman rule, supported by the Buddhistic priesthood, is one long, black catalogue of usurpations, grinding tyrannies, assassinations, and unnatural massacres. There is no protection from immediate execution at the caprice of the king." *

To the East lies the kingdom of Siam, known to the natives as Muang T'hai, "the kingdom of the free," including, besides the original seat of the race, the dependencies of Laos and Camboja, and several tributary Malay states and islands, along the Malayan peninsula, down to the neighbourhood of Singapore. It has an area of 200,000 square miles and a population of about eight millions, of whom two millions are Chinese. The country is very mountainous, the valleys well watered and vegetation very rank everywhere. The people are described as the vainest and most indolent in the East. The gentry smoke, drink and gamble, attend cock-fighting or sail on the river, and the poorer work when driven by necessity. Of Bangkok, the capital, a city of half a million of inhabitants, Bainbridge says: "It would appear that in no city of the world is there so much gambling. Along the business streets every sixth or eighth store is an open den." They are extremely ceremonious, breaches of etiquette being punished with death, and are described as "excelling all Asiatics, in begging, palavering and falsehood." The women are not kept in seclusion, but have considerable liberty. In general they are not expected to live virtuous lives before marriage, but the penalty for immorality afterward is death. They do the most of the work, and are mere drudges. There is much slavery throughout the land, the people of Laos

---

* Bainbridge's "Around the World of Missions."

particularly being noted as slave-hunters. When times are hard, the mandarins organize a regular expedition against the wild tribes in the interior for the capture of slaves, convoys of whom are forwarded to Bangkok and other places.

There is some education among them, and they have books in their old religious or Pali language, written on palm leaf with an iron stylus, but the missionaries have laid the foundation of a better literature, the printing press has been introduced, and the present king, who is entirely progressive in his views, has introduced a general system of education.

The national religion is Buddhism, and it is said that in no country, unless perhaps Thibet, is its sway more complete. It is inwrought in the whole life of the people, and apostasy is considered a crime scarcely less than treason. As to their morals, all that visitors feel it necessary to say is, that they will be found faithfully described in the first chapter of Romans.

Farther East still is Cochin China including the empire of Annam proper, Tonquin and the French Cochin China. It is a long strip of country, along a coast line of 1,240 miles, with a breadth ranging from 372 miles to 50, and an area about the same as Siam. The total population is from ten to twelve millions, besides French Cochin China, which contains 1,487,200, of whom the Europeans number only 1,114.

In this country Buddhism has lost its hold upon the people. The priests, so numerous in other Buddhist lands, are here few and little respected. The writer last quoted says: "The spacious temples of the centuries past have given place to mean little idol houses, where often the people repair to thrash their Buddhas with bamboo sticks if they have not had their desires granted; when more leniently disposed, they will simply turn the idol around with his face to the wall. The population seem to have wearied of the religious principles of Siddhartha on the one hand, and of the frequently imposed philosophy of Confucius on the other, and to have fallen back into a veneration of ancestral and other spirits." He adds that, in a country with a population twice that of Ireland, there is not a single Protestant missionary.

It may be observed, in regard to all the tribes inhabiting the Indo-Chinese peninsula, that, while their religion is nominally Buddhist, it is largely composed of their old systems, with which Buddhism readily entered into alliance. The prevalent one was nature worship, in that form to which the term Animism has been applied, from its ascribing a soul to each object and phenomenon of nature. This is more particularly the case with the wild or mixed races in the interior, of whom some have scarcely the idea of God, make offerings to local genii, and seek to guard their homes from evil spirits by brooms, cotton thread, bunches of herbage, or similar devices, while others, in such emergencies as illness, resort to devil-dancing, to which we shall refer in our next chapter.

To the South-East lies the East Indian or Malay Archipelago, the largest cluster of islands in the world.

It includes Borneo, supposed by some to be larger than New Guinea, in which case it would be, after Australia, the largest island in the world; Sumatra, 1,000 miles long and as large as Great Britain; Celebez and Java, each as large as Ireland, and many others. Excluding New Guinea and the islands farther East, whose inhabitants are of a different stock, they are estimated to contain a population of 34,000,000, who are mostly of the Malay race, the same that inhabits the Malayan peninsula. They were for some time regarded by many as forming a separate variety of the human family, but are now thought to be Mongols, modified by residence in a different climate and by their maritime life. The majority profess Mohammedanism, but, while repeating the formula of that religion in unintelligible Arabic, they still offer their worship to heathen gods, as earnestly as do those who remain avowed heathen.

Passing to the interior, the first Buddhist country which attracts our attention is Thibet, lying on the North of India. It is a rugged tableland, on the average about 15,000 feet above the level of the sea, broken by a succession of mountain ranges, commonly rising to the region of perpetual snow. Between these are valleys usually narrow, but at intervals opening into wider plains. The climate is very rigorous, the cold of winter being extreme and the droughts of summer excessive, so that the country as a whole is not much better than a desert.

To the North of Thibet lies Mongolia. This is a

vast region, but it is thinly peopled. The larger part to the West is a hard, stony desert. Rain falls but rarely, and only in small quantities, so that the only cultivated spots are on the mountains, where the rainfall is greater, or the melting snow is employed for irrigation. What inhabitants it contains are essentially nomadic, their wealth consisting of horned cattle, sheep, horses and camels. Eastern Mongolia, however, which borders on China to the East, is of a different character. Portions in the centre and South-East are extremely mountainous, but it has many valleys of great extent and extremely fertile. The inhabitants are partly agricultural and partly nomadic.

To the North-East lies Manchuria, a country about half the size of China proper, or containing 700,000 square miles, which visitors have described in the highest terms, as possessing an excellent climate, a fertile soil, and vast mineral resources, in gold, silver, lead, copper, iron and coal. The population has long been agricultural.

In the three countries last mentioned a form of Buddhism prevails, known as Lamaism, the word lama denoting a monk. The distinguishing feature of this system is, that it has a hierarchy similar to that of the Church of Rome, and that the head of it, known as the Grand Lama, is at the same time the sole sovereign of Thibet. His political authority is confined to that country, but he is the acknowledged head of the Buddhist Church in Mongolia, and he is partially recognized in the same position in China.

Without entering into a particular description of the religious and moral condition of the several lands under Buddhism, we shall endeavour to give a brief view of the history, principles and working of the system.

SECTION II.—HISTORY AND PRINCIPLES OF BUDDHISM.

The personal name of the founder of this system was Siddhartha, and his family name Gautama, by which he is most commonly known. He is also, throughout the East, distinguished as Sakya Muni and Buddha, both of which are titles, the first meaning the sage of Sakya, the tribe to which he belonged, the latter, the enlightened. Till recently it has been questioned whether there ever was such an individual; and undoubtedly his history, as given by his followers, is in large measure mythical. But the learned are now generally agreed that he was a real personage, and that, amid the mass of legends connected with him, the leading facts of his life may still be gathered. He was born about 600 years before Christ. He was the son of Suddhodana, rajah or king of the Sakya tribe, one of the divisions of the Kshatriya or warrior caste—located at the foot of the Himalayas, a few days' journey North of Benares.

He grew up as other young rajahs, enjoying the luxury of an Eastern court, but early showed a disposition to seclusion and meditation. In particular, his mind became much affected by the prevalence of disease, old age and death around him. How deliverance from these evils could be attained became the absorbing subject of his thoughts, and finally he resolved on a life of ascetism. Accordingly, in his twenty-ninth year, when his wife had just given birth to her first-born son, he tore himself away from all domestic ties, assumed the garb of a mendicant, and with a message to his father, that he would not return till he could bring tidings of deliverance from disease, decay and death, he set out on his weary quest for that object.

His first resort was to the great Brahman teachers; but he soon became dissatisfied with their teachings, or rather, he had already become settled in his conviction of the unsatisfactory nature of their principles. He could, and always did in the main, adopt their views of transmigration; but he saw that this system provided no ultimate rest; that after a succession of births it offered no hope of final deliverance. Farther, he argued against the idea of any merit being found in abstinence from sufficient food, on the ground that in that case the cattle, who only ate grass, would have the highest degree of it; and he objected to sacrifice, that it caused suffering, and that it was thus a seeking good by doing evil. Farther, he held that the gods of the Brahmanical system were no gods, inasmuch as they were represented as having obtained their position by austerities, in the same way as man obtained advancement in his future birth.

Dissatisfied, he retired with five Brahmans to the forests, where he spent six years as a recluse, given to meditation, and afflicting himself with mortifications, the fame of which spread far and wide; but during that time he was unsuccessful in obtaining the object sought. Then his physical strength gave way, and he resorted to better food. But at length, after a fearful mental struggle, as he supposed with tempting demons, light dawned upon him. The four verities, which constituted the way of deliverance, rose clearly before his mind, and he became Buddha, or the enlightened.

Having attained this position himself, his next idea was that others should share in the light; and though at first almost overcome with a sense of the difficulty of bringing men to the knowledge of the truth, yet from that sympathy which led him to subject himself to years of exposure and hardship, and a feeling that all would be in vain, or his object only partially gained, if others were not benefited by it, he resolved to commence the undertaking. He first set out for Benares, the great seat of Brahmanical worship, and began to communicate the new gospel to his old teachers. He soon gained disciples. His own princely bearing; his deep, rich, thrilling voice, such as has distinguished so many successful leaders of men; the reverence which his life of self-abnegation had gained for him; his own powers as a teacher; his deep earnestness and conviction of the truth of his doctrine, favoured by the circumstances in which he propounded them, drew men to his side. Even kings became his followers. But he continued the life of a recluse, travelling from one place to another, subsisting on such food as was given him, for forty-six years, at the end of which time he died, or as the Buddhists say, entered Nirvana in his eightieth year.

In his lifetime he had originated a system of propagandism, and after his death his doctrines continued to spread, so that they became for a time the prevailing religion of a great part of India, particularly in its Northern portions. But Buddhism failed to satisfy the religious cravings of the human heart, and Brahmanism soon rallied. Allying itself to the native religions, it after a time obtained a complete victory, so that Buddhism as a system became nearly extinct in India, although it has left something of its impress upon the dominant system. From India it spread to those countries which we have described in the first part of this chapter as still under the system. But we may say that wherever it became predominant, it was by alliance with the civil power.

PRINCIPLES OF BUDDHISM.

Gautama left no written statement of his views, but his followers after his death endeavoured to collect his teachings. According to them, these were partly doctrinal and partly practical. The fundamental principles of the first were the four great verities, which he discovered under the Bo tree:—1. Suffering exists wherever there is life. 2. The cause of suffering is desire, *i.e.*, a craving for what is only a temporary illusion. 3. Deliverance from suffering, and consequently from life, can only be effected by deliverance from desire, or by obtaining Nirvana. 4. Nirvana can only be obtained by following the method of Buddha.

At the root of the system were two principles:— 1. Buddhist philosophy did not recognise any spiritual existence, any soul in man, or permanent self, separable from the body; and 2. It held, with the Brahmans, the doctrine of transmigration. On the first of these, regarding life as material, it involved decay. Buddha's last words are reported to have been: "Beloved, that which causes life causes also decay and death. Never forget this; let your minds be filled with this truth. I called you to make it known to you." Thus, as long as there is life there must be sorrow. While man is, he must be miserable. The only way of deliverance is, by getting quit of life itself. Of course, as Christians, we deny the fundamental principle of this system, that life is necessarily sorrow. But in the uncertainty of life and other miseries of the state of society in which Buddha lived, and with the repulsive aspects of life in other worlds, as exhibited in the Brahmanical doctrine of transmigration, we need not wonder at his adopting such a pessimist view of life.

But if the extinction of life was the object to be aimed at, and if all life is material, we would conclude that the end would be gained by death. Against this the doctrine of transmigration interposed. According to this, our condition in this life is determined by *karma*. The word means deeds, and it represents the aggregate of a man's conduct, or the character so formed in some previous state of existence. And the same in this life will necessitate our birth in another, and determine our condition there; so that it becomes necessary to get rid not only of the present, but of all life. According to this doctrine, there is a series of hells for the evil and heavens for the good, in none of which can they permanently remain, but must pass into another with the same process of decay and death. To be quit of all this should be the aim of all men. This was Nirvana, the Buddhist's goal.

But how was this to be gained? Pain was occasioned by affection and desire, and therefore all affections and desires must be extinguished, and thus entire quiescence be reached with entire annihilation. It is probable that the teaching of Buddhism in regard to Nirvana led to the Brahmans adopting the idea of absorption into Brahm, since taught as the ultimate object to which men's desires are to be directed.

It must be observed, that in all this there was no recognition of a Supreme Being. The Brahmans had taught that their gods had attained their position by austerities. From this view Buddha concluded that they were unworthy to be worshipped. They now occupied the heavens as the fish the sea, men and animals the earth, but they were liable to decay, and might yet become men or beasts. Besides, to suppose a divine being moved by worship, was to suppose him influenced by desire, and thus liable to decay. Thus, if he did not deny God altogether, he constructed a system of the universe in which he had no place. The atheistic character of Buddhism originally is admitted by all who have carefully examined the subject. In all its teaching and in all its efforts, it did not recognize the idea of reconciliation with God, either as to its necessity or the means by which it was to be attained.

But Buddha has received more credit, and deservedly so, for his teaching on morals. The question still remained, according to his scheme, How was desire to be extinguished and men reach Nirvana? The method, according to the fourth verity, was by the following four paths, applicable to all:—1st, right vision or faith; 2nd, right judgment or thoughts; 3rd, right language; 4th, right actions. Under these the precepts he laid down were five in a negative form—not to kill, extending even to animal life; not to steal; not to commit adultery; not to lie—this extending to the use of improper language; and not to use strong drink: and, positively, he enjoined six virtues—charity, purity, patience, courage, contemplation, science. The best way, however, to attain it, was by becoming a recluse, and he laid down a variety of precepts for the regulation of the conduct of such. But the laity he urged to the fulfilment of these duties, so that if they could not become recluses, they might hope for a happier birth in their next condition of existence, and thus reach so far toward Nirvana.

In all this Buddha appears but as the representative of the natural reaction of the times against the Brahmanism prevalent. By that system stress was laid upon austerities and penances, or upon sacrifices and worship, which had become a mere form. Religion and morals had parted company. The priests showed no example of morality in their persons, nor was personal purity connected with the service of God in the lives of the worshippers. It was therefore a natural tendency that Buddha followed, in going in the opposite direction and insisting on the discharge of relative duties, and the performance of works of benevolence toward all animated being.

In another respect his teaching is to be admired, though it was really the working of the spirit of the age. He rejected caste, which had become an intolerable tyranny. The one way of deliverance he exhibited as equally open to the Sudra as to the Brahman, and both were equally welcome to his teaching.

But while giving him the credit due for this, we must at the same time point out that while his moral precepts were good, and may be taken as evidence that the law is written on the heart of man, his system, as a system of morality, had a fatal defect at the foundation. It had no place for conscience. It did not regard duty as duty, or right as right. It started with the idea of deliverance from misery, not sin, as the great evil. It aimed at morality and commanded benevolence, not as good in themselves, but as means of attaining to nothingness. The whole was, therefore, a system of selfishness.

Such is a brief view of Buddhism as originally propounded. We cannot follow it in the great variety of speculation into which it has since run, nor trace its developments in different lands, but must endeavour to give a general view of its practical working, inasmuch as in this case, as with Brahmanism, the system, as it appears in the writings of its first exponents, presents marked contrasts with the system which missionaries meet in actual operation in the life of the peoples subject to it.

SECTION III.—PRACTICAL WORKING OF BUDDHISM.

IDOLATRY.

We have already said that Buddha recognized no God. His system therefore failed to satisfy the religious sense in man. Human nature craves a god, and though Buddhism spread over a great part of India, and was embraced by multitudes as a relief from priestly or caste tyranny, their souls were unsatisfied.. In reality they never gave up their old idols. Even yet in Ceylon, where the system has been in full operation for twenty centuries, its adherents show the void that it leaves in the heart. "The people look to Buddhism for deliverance as to the future world. By its instrumentality, they suppose that they can gain merit; but for present assistance, when the burden of affliction is heavy upon them, their resort is to the demon priest, with his incantations and sacrifices."*

When his followers renounced their ancestral gods, they soon gave him a place above them, and rendered him a worship similar to what they had rendered to

---

* "Hardy's Legends and Theories of the Buddhists," quoted by Robson.

them. Legends representing him as possessed of superhuman power, gathered around his memory, and he came to be regarded as possessed of omniscience and supreme power. As they express it, he is "the joy of the whole world, the dewa of dewas, the brahma of brahmas, the very compassionate, more powerful than the most powerful, able to bestow Nirvana on him who only softly pronounces his name, or gives in his name a few grains of rice."* Images of him, which dwarf all the idols of Hindooism, were erected in their temples. Brahma and Indra were repudiated, but the former was represented as paying homage to the discarded robe of Buddha, and the latter as coming from heaven to secure the dish from which he had eaten, that he might set it up as an object of worship in his heavenly abode.

They also deified various inferior beings, giving them a place above the demigods of mythology, and now Buddhist temples are crowded with images, sometimes to the number of 500, thus forming pantheons in which saints, heroes, and devils are worshipped, and to these representations in brass, wood, or mud, the mass of the worshippers bow in worship. Buddha himself felt the want of an object of worship. One of his friends having been killed by his enemies, he preserved some relics of him with a care that amounted to devotion, and thus introduced the worship of relics, so that now in Buddhist temples the chief object of religious veneration is a tomb supposed

* Hardy.

to contain some remains of this kind. Thus the system, which distinguished itself by denying God altogether, ended in the worship of the tooth or bone of a dead man, or even his discarded garment.

In all the countries beyond India to which Buddhism has extended, it allied itself with the old forms of heathenism, which continued to retain their power but little changed over the minds of the inhabitants. In Thibet it allowed the worship of the genii of the rivers, woods, hills, etc., and something of the same state of things continues to the present day throughout the whole Indo-Chinese peninsula. In China it readily combined with all the old worship of the inhabitants, rendering offerings, not only to ancestors, but to evil as well as good spirits, and in Japan it accommodated itself with equal facility to the Shintoism of that country. Thus the types of Buddhism in all these countries differ from the original and from one another, but all are overlaid with superstition, as degrading as those against which it originally protested.

FORMALISM.

As we have seen, Buddhism rose as a protest against the soulless ceremonial of the Brahman worship, and having in contrast with it set up works, as what should engage attention, we might have expected that it would have saved its votaries from formalism, but the fact is patent at the present day, that in no other religion does the worship consist of such utterly unmeaning forms. Other Churches have had their prayers in a language not understood by the common people, but the words constantly on the lips of the Buddhist are not understood by anybody. "*Om mane padne hum*" are the first words the child is taught to lisp, and the last with which the soul leaves the body. "The wanderer," we are told, "murmurs them on his way, the herdsman beside his cattle, the matron at her daily tasks, the monk in all the stages of contemplation; they form at once a cry of battle and a shout of victory. They are to be read, wherever the Lama Church has spread, upon banners, upon rocks, upon trees, upon walls, upon monuments of stone, upon household utensils, upon human skulls and skeletons."* And yet the most learned cannot agree as to their meaning, or whether they have any.

Indeed, as the system had no place for prayer, the use of them is as a sort of charm. Here Buddhism has produced something entirely novel, and which has never been introduced into any other religion—the praying machine. "These mysterious words," says Dr. Dods, "are written or printed many times over on long scrolls of paper, which are wound within a small brass cylinder. This cylinder rotates upon an axis, and as often as it is set spinning, so many prayers are said. These cylinders are carried by the lamas, who keep them spinning while they converse with you; they are fixed in the walls of houses, and as often as any of the family passes, another turn is given to the wheel; they are also provided with fans, and set on

---

* Heeley and Kœppen, quoted by Dods.

the tops of houses, where the wind keeps them moving, or in a stream, which drives the praying mills for behoof of the community."

MONASTICISM.

Buddha, while laying down a code of precepts for all classes, and admitting those who in this life brought up a family and lived a life of honest industry to an advance in the next, yet reserved his highest blessings for the man of contemplation, who passed through the world in disregard of all earthly interests. Hence he laid down a code of the most rigidly ascetic character, for the guidance of all who wished to attain Nirvana. His doctrine tended to encourage the practice. If all life was evil, then the course of the celibate was better than that of the married man. Hence, wherever Buddhism has prevailed, there has been an enormous development of monasticism. Idle mendicants swarm everywhere. In Siam, one in forty of the whole population, making 200,000 in the empire, are vagabonds of this character. Of these Sir John Bowring, who made a special study of the religion of Siam, says, " A bonze seems to care nothing about the condition of those who surround him; he makes no effort for their elevation or improvement. He scarcely reproves their sin or encourages their virtues. He is self-satisfied with his own superior holiness, and would not move his finger to remove any mass of human misery."

But the greatest development of the system has

been in Mongolia and Thibet. In portions of the former, the lamas, as the monks are called, include one-third of the male population. Indeed, Mr. Gilmour, a missionary of the London Missionary Society, who spent some years in missionary labours in that country, estimates the proportion even as high as 60 per cent. One monastery is said to contain 30,000, and several others in both countries number their inmates by thousands. The withdrawment of so much of the population from industrial pursuits, and their exemption from taxation, is a terrible hindrance to the progress of the country. Their aim is to live by their religious office. Many do so, and those who cannot, seek to do as little work as possible. Farther, their spiritual influence is a fearful engine of oppression. For all their services large fees are exacted, it being held that their prayers are valueless without pay. On the occasion of a death, for the deliverance of the soul from purgatory, a family previously living in abundance may be robbed of all they possess.

Moreover, the ignorance and corruption, which have so often been the ultimate issue of monasticism, are here displayed in their worst forms, rendering the system, as a late explorer has said, "the most frightful curse of the country." "Lamaism, with its shaven priests, its bells and rosaries, its images and holy water, its abbots and monks of many grades, its confessional and purgatory, and its worship of the double virgin, so strongly resembles Romanism, that the first Catholic missionaries thought that it must be an imitation by the devil of the religion of Christ; and that the resemblance is not in externals only, is shown by the present state of Thibet—the oppression of all thought, the idleness and corruption of the monks, the despotism of the Government and the poverty and beggary of the people." *

In Mongolia, according to Mr. Gilmour, the corruption of morals among the lamas is frightful. He says: "The great sinners in Mongolia are the lamas, the great centres of wickedness are the temples." A large proportion of these men are put under vows when children from six to ten years of age. At that time, pleased with the honour of wearing the red cloak of the lama, they can have little idea of the obligations under which they come. Hence afterward, as he says: " They cannot get free from their vows—they cannot keep them, so they break them repeatedly and systematically; their conscience is seared; and now that they are started, they do not stop with merely violating vows they cannot keep, but having cast aside restraint and acquired momentum in sin, they go on to the most unthought-of wickedness. Thus it comes that the great lama centres are the great centres of sin. The headquarters of Mongol Buddhism is Urga, where Satan's seat is. If you go there, you will be warned never to go out after dark, except you are well armed; and a foreigner, who knew something of the place, remarked that he believed that the lamas there lived in the daily practice of all the sins known among men,

---

* "Ency. Brit.," Vol. IV., 438.

murder alone excepted." "The encampment of the Supreme Lama of Mongolia is reputed to be the most supremely wicked place in the whole of that wide country."

POSITION OF WOMAN.

A word only can be said regarding the position which Buddhism assigns to woman. One of its fundamental principles is that there is no hope for her except of being born a man in the next birth. Her sex is considered the proof, and the punishment of sins committed in a former state. Grudgingly, she is allowed the position of a nun, but with no prospect of attaining Nirvana. In one respect woman is worse under the refined systems of Brahmanism and Buddhism than under the rude and, it may be, gross superstition of savages. Under the latter she is abused and treated as a drudge, but under the former, her degradation is made part of their religious creed, and thus, while receiving in this life treatment corresponding, she is cut off from hope in the future.

MORALITY.

We have already mentioned, that Buddha inculcated a comparatively high morality, and also benevolence to living creatures; but his system has proved an entire failure as to moral power, and this for the reason already stated, if for no other, that it was founded entirely on selfishness. According to it, the only reason for performing any good act, is the merit that will be thus acquired. "In conversation with a Buddhist priest," says Bainbridge, "I asked what could be his motive in saving his own brother from drowning." He replied, "that there would be great merit in it." " I have tried," he adds, "to fathom the motive depths of many Buddhists, and, in proportion as they have imbibed the spirit of their system, the more utterly destitute they seemed to be of any leading thought beyond themselves, for either this life or the life to come. "Buddhism pays no attention to the moral qualities of an action. Lying, stealing, and adultery are to be avoided, not because they are wrong or injure our neighbour—of such considerations the system takes no account—but because whosoever refrains from such acts, gains so much merit, and takes a step toward Nirvana. The mind is thus trained to act solely from a regard to self-interest, and the very foundations of morality are destroyed. Thus, too, Buddhism has no proper conception of guilt. Sin is only a misfortune or the result of deeds done in a former state.

In Mongolia Mr. Gilmour testifies that intelligent people among them will generally admit, that the system has utterly failed to purify the heart and to produce the fruits of holy living. "Its practical effect is to delude its votaries as to actual guilt, to sear their consciences as with a hot iron, to call the wicked righteous, and send men down to the grave with a lie in their right hand." He says that the most religious Mongols will steal without sense of shame, and lie while saying their prayers; that the lamas are sometimes notorious thieves, and do not lose caste in consequence. "The influence of the wickedness of the lamas," he adds, "is most hurtful. It is well known. They sin not only among themselves, but sow their evil among the people. The people look upon them as sacred, and of course think that they may do as the lamas do. Thus the corrupting influence spreads, and the state of Mongolia to-day, as regards uprightness and morality, is such as makes the heart more sick the more one knows of it."

Equally has the system failed to induce practical benevolence. The founder of it seems to have been influenced by a genuine spirit of philanthropy, though his principles would indicate that he did not appreciate its true nature. He strongly enjoined upon all his disciples kindness to all creatures. Hence his followers show a careful regard for animal life, and Brahmanism has adopted the same idea. But the same principle of self-interest rules them in this as in all their actions. The giving food to a starving wretch, equally with the act of a mother ministering to a sick child, is only regarded as a means of gaining so many merit marks on the book of the death god. The actual result is, that inhumanity is as characteristic of Buddhism as immorality. "The real and invincible objection to Buddhism," says Sir John Bowring, "is its selfishness, its disregard of others, its deficiency in all the promptings of sympathy and benevolence." A Thibetan will brush a seat before sitting on it, lest he should kill an insect, but murder his prisoners of war in cold blood. Priests will feed apes and sacred pigs in their temples, and leave men and women to die of starvation on the streets, and their bodies to be devoured by dogs in the very neighbourhood of their sacred buildings.

An attempt has been made to glorify Buddhism as "the light of Asia." "The darkness of Asia" would be a truer description. No religion on that continent has left its votaries in a lower moral condition. The teaching of Confucius deserves far higher honour than that of Buddha. He did inculcate moral duty as duty, and sought to found a state upon it, and so far succeeded that his system has been a conservative element in Chinese society for long centuries. The old Rig-Veda of the Hindoos afforded materials for a better reformation than that which Siddhartha originated. The Karens and the hill tribes of the Indo-Chinese peninsula, still following their old rude native worship, or sometimes seeming to be without worship altogether, have more virtues and fewer vices, are more open to better moral teaching, than the Burmese and Siamese votaries of Buddhism. Mohammedanism did not take away the principle of duty, and even Brahmanism did not thoroughly overlay conscience. But Buddhism—gild the carcase as you may, approach to it from any side—only reveals a mass of corruption, the hugest and most offensive in the nostrils of purity the world has ever seen.*

---

*The authorities on which we have principally relied in this account of Buddha and Buddhism are—Robson's "Hindooism and Christianity," Dods' "Buddha and Christ," Bainbridge's "Around the World of Missions," Gilmour's "Among the Mongols," and articles in the "Encyclopædia Britannica."

CHAPTER III.

SHAMANISM, AND THE DEVIL-WORSHIPPERS OF ASIA.

"They sacrificed unto devils, not to God."—Deut. xxxii. 17.
"Yea, they sacrificed their sons and their daughters unto devils."—Psalm cvi. 37.

"THE things which the Gentiles sacrifice, they sacrifice to devils, and not to God," says the Apostle Paul, in writing to the Corinthians (1 Epis. x. 10). As the Greeks used the original word "demon," to denote good spirits as well as evil, it might be that he did not mean that their services were directly to the latter, although the tenor of the passage seems to teach this. It is possible, too, that in these words, as well as in those of Moses and the Psalmist, at the head of this chapter, the reference is to all idol worship, which, being from the instigation of Satan, might be said to be a service to him. But it is certain that, quite distinct from those forms of idolatry in which the objects represented by the idols are regarded as more or less beneficent, there has been underlying various systems of paganism the idea that evil spirits are to be appeased and their wrath deprecated by appropriate offerings. It is found in the fetich worship of Africa, and in much of the religious services of the natives of the South Seas, as well as of the Indians in the Western parts of North America.

But farther, the worship of many of our race in the past has been, and of a number still is, directly and systematically rendered to evil spirits, and to them alone. This forms the basis of the system known as Shamanism, though it also implies the idea of Shamans, or sacred men, through whom the power of these beings is managed or controlled. This was the religion of the whole Tartar race in the interior of Asia, before it was supplanted by Buddhism and Mohammedanism; but even where the former has become predominant, the same idea largely moulds the religious feelings of the races who have adopted it. Traces of it are still found in some of the services even of the Chinese. It still prevails in those portions of that continent to which these two systems have not extended. It is the religion, for example, of Siberia, a region nearly as large as all Europe—subject, indeed, to great extremes of heat and cold, but now regarded as a country of vast resources, though at present very thinly peopled.

Bodies of devil-worshippers are still to be found in various other places. Layard gives an interesting account of a tribe of them, known as Yesidees, in the neighbourhood of Mosul, and heard of others in other places. These generally recognize the existence of a supreme being, but they do not offer him any direct prayer or sacrifice, regarding him as too good to do them any harm. The name of the evil spirit they never mention, and any allusion to it so vexes them, that it is said that they have put to death persons who wantonly outraged their feelings by its use. So far is their dread of offending him carried, that they carefully avoid using any word resembling in sound the name of Satan, or the Arabic word for accursed. When they speak of the devil, they speak of him with reverence as Melek el Kout, the mighty angel, or Melek Taous, king Peacock, in accordance with which they have a bronze figure of a bird, which the Sheikh was careful to explain they regarded as a symbol, not as an idol, but which as such they treated with great veneration.

Mr. Layard says: "They believe Satan to be the chief of the angelic host, now suffering punishment for rebellion against the divine will, but still all-powerful, and to be restored hereafter to his high estate in the celestial hierarchy. He must be conciliated they say, for as he now has the means of doing evil to mankind, so will he hereafter have the power of rewarding them. Next to Satan, but inferior to him in might and wisdom, are seven archangels, who exercise a great influence over the world."

But the best known devil-worshippers are in India. They are generally living among the hills and are supposed to be the remnants of the aboriginal tribes who inhabited the country previous to the arrival of the Aryan race. Brahmanism, from its tendency to absorb other systems, has adopted some of the practices of these aboriginal tribes, and their system has received some modifications from it. But among some, at least, it still remains a genuine devil or demon worship, perhaps the most unmixed that is to be found anywhere.

The Rev. S. Mateer, missionary of the London Missionary Society, in his work, "Travancore and its People," has given an account of the devil-worshippers in that province, from which we obtain the following information:—

They have an idea of a supreme being, but do not present any worship to him, as they think he will do them no harm. They do not, however, as the Yesidees, give their worship solely to Satan as the one great evil spirit, but to a variety of minor ones. These are all supposed to be influenced by the spirit of malice, and each in his own way to be seeking to injure the human race. They are believed to be numerous and active, to be met with everywhere, and their influence to be felt in every evil that men suffer. There is a great variety among them. One greatly dreaded is named Madan, which means "he who is like a cow,"* who is supposed to cause sudden illness to men and cattle, but he also appears in various forms, in each of which he employs his powers in doing mischief to men. Others are supposed to frequent places where bodies are burnt or buried; another, called Kumili Madan, "bubble devil," is supposed to dance on the surface of the water; while another,

---

* Compare representations still seen among us of Satan with horns and hoofs.

called the "old man of the three roads," is supposed to lurk where several roads meet, and all with the design to injure those who may fall into their hands.

They are supposed to be of both sexes, but the female demons are regarded as the most cruel and malicious. The principal of them, however, is a form of Kali, the wife of Siva, the god of destruction, and is supposed to have been introduced from the Brahmanical system. She is represented as delighted with blood, cruelty and lust. It is in honour of her that hook-swinging and other tortures are adopted by devotees. Formerly, at one of her shrines, a young woman in her first pregnancy was offered in sacrifice. Her head was struck off with one blow of a sword and rolled at the foot of the image, which was also sprinkled with her blood. "She is often represented by the hideous figure of a woman with an infant in her hand which she is in the act of devouring and crushing between her teeth. This terrible image is habitually worshipped by thousands of poor ignorant mothers of India."

In addition, the spirits of wicked men who have met with a violent death by hanging, drowning, etc., are supposed to become malignant spirits wandering about seeking to injure, and especially haunting the place where they had met their end. Hence arose the strange custom which continued till 1862, that criminals executed by hanging should be hamstrung at the moment of being thrown off. Hence they are actually worshipped after death. A noted robber was long thus honoured at Tinnevelly.

"The minor superstitions connected with demon-worship," Mr. Mateer says, "are well-nigh innumerable; they enter into all the feelings and are associated with the whole life of these people. Every disease, accident or misfortune is attributed to the agency of the devils, and great caution is exercised to avoid rousing their fury."

Devil temples are very numerous through that country. They are generally mere sheds, a few yards in length, open at one end, and generally empty. In reality images form no part of demon worship, and where they exist they seem to have been introduced from Brahmanism. In front of these buildings stands a small obelisk, or pyramidal erection, four or five feet high, generally built of brick and stuccoed, the design of which is not known.

The offerings are very varied, generally of such articles of food or drink, not forgetting arrack, as are most esteemed by the people themselves. But through all Southern India the animal sacrifices are deemed the most important. These demons are supposed to be thirsting for human blood, and doubtless human sacrifices were formerly offered, as they are said to be still in secret among the Khonds; but in general they are believed to be propitiated by the sacrifices of animals, such as sheep, goats, fowls and pigs, which are offered on all important occasions.

Great festivals are held, generally annually, at some of the most renowned temples. A missionary thus describes what he saw at one of these: "About 50,000 people, it is believed, assembled there, and were found offering goats and fowls, and performing different vows to the goddess. We saw hundreds of children of both sexes, some carried in the arms and others led by their parents to perform some ceremonies, crying out and shedding tears through pain. When we went near to the pagoda, a boy was brought by several relations, with tom-toms (drums) and dancing. Then a goldsmith, who was there ready with a large needle and small rattans, came forward and pierced through both his sides with the needle; when the boy cried aloud through pain, all the relations made a terrible noise. The smith then drew a rattan through the holes on both sides, bringing it round the back, and gave both ends of the rattans to them. They then led the boy round the pagoda."

Connected with this is *devil-dancing*, the object of which is to become possessed by the demon. Another missionary thus describes one which he saw: "When the preparations are completed, and the devil-dance is about to commence, the music is at first comparatively slow, and the dancer seems impassive and sullen, and either stands still or moves about in gloomy silence. Gradually, as the music becomes quicker and louder, his excitement begins to rise. Sometimes, to help him to work himself into a frenzy, he uses medicated draughts, cuts and lacerates his flesh till the blood comes, lashes himself with a huge whip, presses a burning torch to his breast, drinks the blood which flows from his own wounds, or drinks the blood of the sacrifice, putting the throat of the decapitated goat to his mouth.* Then, as if he had acquired new life, he begins to brandish his staff of bells, and to dance with a quick but wild, unsteady step. Suddenly the afflatus descends, there is no mistaking that glare or those frantic leaps. He snorts, he stares, he gyrates. The demon has now taken bodily possession of him; and though he retains the power of utterance and of motion, both are under the demon's control, and his separate consciousness is in abeyance. The bystanders signalize the event by raising a long shout, attended with a peculiar vibrating noise, caused by the motion of the hand and tongue, or the tongue alone. The devil-dancer is now worshipped as a present deity, and every bystander consults him respecting his disease, his wants, the welfare of his absent relatives, the offerings to be made for the accomplishment of his wishes, and, in short, respecting everything for which superhuman knowledge is supposed to be available. As the devil-dancer acts to admiration the part of a maniac, it requires some experience to enable a person to interpret his dubious or unmeaning replies, his muttered voices and uncouth gestures; but the wishes of the parties who consult him help them greatly to interpret his meaning."

Well might Mr. Mateer say of this system: "We cannot well conceive any superstition more wicked or revolting in character, or more degrading and pernicious in its influence, than the baleful devil-wor-

---

* Compare Psa. xvi. 4.

ship, which we have attempted to describe. It is, of course, in a still higher degree than idolatry, a daring crime against the God of heaven—a rejection of His authority, and a deliberate attempt to set up Satan in the throne which the Most High alone should occupy." "And as to moral influence, it is evident that it hardens the heart and increases cruelty, covetousness, worldliness, and other evil passions."

CHAPTER IV.

CHINA, HER PEOPLE AND HER RELIGIONS.

"Behold these shall come far: and, lo, these from the north and from the west; and these from *the land of Sinim.*" (Isa. xlix. 12.)

IN considering the state of the heathen at the present time, China and her people must claim special attention. Indeed, in any view we can take, either of the land itself, or the number, character, history and condition of its inhabitants, we will find them worthy of the thoughtful consideration of any person interested in the past or future of our race.

SECTION I.—COUNTRY AND PEOPLE.

COUNTRY.

As to the country itself, China proper covers an area of 1,340,000 square miles, more than eleven times that of Great Britain and Ireland, or seven times that of France. And if we include the countries in subordination to her government and forming the Chinese Empire, the extent will be more than three times as great, being greater than that of all Europe, and embracing one-eleventh of the whole surface of the earth, stretching through seventy degrees of longitude and forty of latitude, with a sea coast four thousand miles long, and a circuit equal to half the circumference of the globe.

It has every variety of scenery, from sea level to the line of perpetual snow. It has one plain greater by a half than the German Empire. One river is larger than the Mississippi, and drains a basin larger than the republic of Mexico; while another is three times the length of the Rhine. So varied is its climate, that it has been said that every plant on the earth might find a congenial habitat on some part of its surface, and every animal thrive in some one or other of its valleys, mountains or waters. Its soil yields every variety of product, while its coal-fields are twenty times the size of those of Europe, and these lie side by side with the most valuable ores of iron and other minerals, practically untouched. Such a country, the more it is studied, must awaken the deepest interest in the minds alike of the scientist, the political economist, the statesman and the Christian.

POPULATION.

But the interest which the country excites fades before a view of its people. Who can realize their numbers? Much discussion has taken place regarding the estimates that have been made on this point. But the best authorities now believe that China contains a population of 400,000,000 souls,* or over one-fourth

---

* As the territory of China is eleven times that of Great Britain and Ireland, if the latter contained a population of 36,000,000 they

of the whole inhabitants of the earth, and about one-half of the whole heathen. If all the inhabitants of the world were to pass before us, every fourth man would be a Chinaman, every fourth child born owns a Chinese mother, and every fourth soul that crosses the dark river left its earthly home in China. Their number is one-third greater than that of all Europe, and exceeds that of the four continents of North and South America, Africa and Oceanica combined. Of these, 33,000 die daily, 1,000,000 every month, and as many as live in the whole Dominion of Canada are buried every four months, while the living, if joined hand to hand, would girdle the earth at the Equator ten times over.

THEIR ANTIQUITY.

A feeling of positive awe comes over us as we contemplate their antiquity. They were a settled people a thousand years before Rome was founded, or the earliest authentic date in Grecian history. They rivalled the Egyptians in literature and knowledge, when Moses studied in their schools; and before Abraham left Ur of the Chaldees, their astronomers had made observations of the heavenly bodies, which, it is said, have been verified by modern scientists. Their history goes back forty centuries, past the days of the kings of Israel, almost to the time of the dis-

---

would only be peopled in the same proportion. But the testimony of travellers who have visited the interior of China is, that it is more densely peopled than these countries, so that the estimate above given of her population is probably not an exaggeration.

persion of mankind after the Flood, during which time Egypt, Assyria, Babylon, Persia, Greece, and Rome have risen, culminated and fallen. No nation on earth has maintained anything like such a continuous existence. The sites of other great empires may show the same country, but the people are different. The Egypt of the Khedive has no connection, except that of the soil, with the Egypt of the Pharaohs. But the Chinese civilization may be traced back through all these ages in an unbroken line. The laws which were codified two thousand years ago, revised at regular intervals, rule her to-day.

THEIR ACHIEVEMENTS.

Nor are we less struck by their achievements. Here is a people who in the days of Abraham had built embankments on their rivers, draining large areas and bringing them under profitable cultivation—who had built their great wall, the greatest work ever constructed by human hands, over two centuries before Christ was born—who before that era had dug canals, and have now 2,000, one of them the longest in the world, irrigating every part of the land, and forming water communication through all their territories—who were dressed in silk when the inhabitants of Britain painted themselves blue, and sailed in their willow canoes—who had discovered gunpowder about the date of the Christian era, and invented firearms as early as the reign of Edward I.—who manufactured paper 1,200 years before the art was known in Europe

—who used the magnet before the birth of Christ, and from whom Europeans probably derived their first knowledge of it—who had invented printing 800 years before Gutenberg was born, and who even yet, in the manufacture of porcelain and various textile fabrics, in some respects surpass European and American workmen.

Here, too, is a people who, at a very early period, had seized the idea, that only as the mind was furnished with knowledge and trained in virtue, did man rise above his fellows, and who have had a universal system of day schools for centuries—with millions able to read and write, and education more widely diffused, at least among the male sex, than in almost every other country—with a literature of overwhelming extent, and a civil service dependant upon educational attainment, decided by competitive examination, and open to every child in the empire who can win literary distinction.

THEIR FUTURE.

This people, the most industrious in the world, and unsurpassed in shrewd practical sagacity, will undoubtedly become the dominant race in the East. The population is overflowing, and already they are finding their way to the regions around. An absurd superstition for the present, in some measure, arrests their colonizing capacity. Let that once be shaken, and they will not only occupy the sparsely-populated adjoining regions of Asia, making the desert to blossom as the rose, but will pour in overwhelming numbers into the isles of the Pacific, and over our own continent. Nay, more; the time will come when they will be found, not merely competing with the labouring classes of Christendom but as merchants, maintaining an honorable rivalry with Europeans and Americans in Liverpool and London, Paris and New York, San Francisco and Montreal. The moral and religious condition of such a people must engage particular attention even in such a brief sketch as the present.

SECTION II.—THEIR RELIGIONS.

There are three systems of religion acknowledged in China: Confucianism, Taouism, and Buddhism.*

CONFUCIANISM.

The first derives its name from Confucius, which is the Latinized form of the name Kung Fu-tze, meaning the philosopher or master Kung. He was born about the year 550 B.C., about a hundred years before Socrates, and near the commencement of the Babylonish captivity. At that time the kingdom of China was comparatively small, both in extent and population. The constitution was feudal, there being a number of petty states under subordinate rulers, who for centuries had been contending with one another. Misrule was chronic, under which the masses were in

---

* This is, of course, besides Mohammedanism, which does not come within our present subject.

misery, often suffering famine. Polygamy, with the low state of woman, and the many restraints laid upon her, led to a series of intrigues, quarrels, and murders impossible to detail, while religious belief had become feeble or had disappeared. "The world," says his disciple Mencius, "had fallen into decay and right principles had disappeared. Perverse discourses and oppressive deeds were waxen rife. Ministers murdered their rulers, and sons their fathers. Confucius was frightened by what he saw and undertook the work of reformation."

The course which he took for this end was in contrast with what has been frequently adopted in the East, by men who have been moved by the evils of the times. He never thought of retiring from society and following the life of a recluse, nor did he give himself up to speculation, so congenial to some Easterns, and by which sometimes their reformers have allowed themselves to be absorbed. On the contrary, he gave his attention to practical reform. During the greatest part of his active life he held office under Government, and, seeing how much of the evil under which men were labouring arose from the wickedness of those in authority, the first idea for which he worked was obtaining a good government. His ideal was, the ruler the father of his people, and they rendering to him obedience with the implicit submission of a child. Subordinate to this, he laid stress on four other relationships—those of husband and wife, father and child, elder brother and younger, and friends. The first four involved rule on the one side and submission on the other. But the rule should be in righteousness and sincerity. Between friends the obligations were mutual. It was in regard to this last relationship that he laid down the principle of the golden rule, at least in the negative form, "Whatsoever ye would that men should not do to you, do ye not to them."

In regard to the duties of these relationships, the chief importance was attached to filial piety. Without this, none of the virtues belonging to the others could be expected. With the soul inspired and the life regulated by this principle, every duty would be discharged, the whole man renovated, and society established in righteousness and safety. The duty was enjoined, not only in youth when children are dependant on parents as their natural protectors, but was to continue as long as they lived. Nor was this reverence to be confined to the present life. From the earliest period of Chinese history, religious worship had been rendered to the spirits of departed ancestors. This, doubtless, began with the natural tributes of respect which affection pays to deceased friends, or the honours which communities render to departed heroes, but ultimately became a real worship. Confucius did not originate the practice, but his system confirmed it, and did much to give it that hold which it has ever since had upon the people of China.

In the state of society then existing, Confucius saw all the duties of these relationships violated, but he held that human nature was originally virtuous, and only led astray by evil influence from without; and he had such confidence in the power of example, that he believed that if he could only get the ruler to act upon these principles, the people would follow in their spheres. He set himself, therefore, to establish the model state, and hoped that, by so reforming the one in which he was a minister, its influence would extend in every direction, till the whole kingdom should be brought under the same beneficent principle. He laboured diligently for this end, and he is worthy of honour for his efforts to remedy the evils of the times, particularly by urging upon those in authority the duties of benevolence and righteousness, and the importance of their example in the community. But he failed. The prince, whose prime minister he was, having shown a disposition to sensual indulgence, he resigned his position and spent the most of his remaining days in wandering. But returning to his native state, he spent the close of his life in discoursing on ceremonies and studying philosophy, and died disappointed and despairing.

But after his death he became the object of unbounded admiration, which has continued to the present day. By all Chinese he is regarded as the model of humanity, and as the infallible teacher of mankind. The Five Classics, being the books of which he was the editor or author, and four other works, compiled by his followers soon after his death, are with them the standard of all truth. In regard to every new doctrine the question with them is, whether it is taught in these books. If it is, it is true; if it is not, it is useless; and if it is contrary to their teaching, it is false. And their faith in these documents is far more implicit than that of Christians in their Bible.

It will thus be seen that Confucius was in reality no teacher of religion. His system was one entirely of ethics and politics, which, in fact, he made his religion. From it everything spiritual and divine was excluded. He sometimes speaks of himself as having a divine mission, but in general his teaching is free from any reference to anything beyond what is seen and temporal. In the oldest Chinese writings, which he regarded with intense veneration, there are references to a great personal ruler, who orders the course both of nature and providence. But with Confucius there is only the idea of a vague, impersonal heaven, or perhaps the notion, prevalent in other Eastern cosmogonies, of the heaven as the male, and the earth as the female principle, from which all matter is produced. But in general in his teaching he simply ignored a superior power or a future retribution. He performed reverently and to the letter the services prescribed to the spirits of the departed, and to other spirits; but he did not regard them as necessary. When asked as to wisdom, his reply was, "To give one's self earnestly to the duties due to men, and while respecting spiritual beings, to keep aloof from them—that may be called wisdom." When one of his disciples asked him how he was to serve spiritual beings, he replied, "Not being able to serve men, how can you serve spirits." And as to the future, his teaching was equally non-committal: "While you do not know life, what can you know about death?"

Thus the system of Confucius was one of pure secularism or agnosticism. He sought to build up morality and social order, with only the sanction of the consequences to ourselves or our successors in the present life. If there was a future, he gave no heed to it, and he drew no motives either from the hope of reward or the fear of punishment in another state. His morality itself was defective, especially in the fact that he never assailed polygamy. This in itself was enough to frustrate his persistent efforts to remedy the evils of his time. And then he recognized no progress, and aimed at no better future. His model was the example of the great men of the Chinese past, and he sought only to have men conform to what they had attained.

TAOUISM.

At the same period with Confucius arose Laou-tze, the founder of the system known as Taouism. He went to the opposite extreme, both as to practical duty and religious teaching. He professed contempt for worldly greatness and domestic happiness, placing the chief good in mental abstraction. His commentator tells us that his scheme of philosophy consists in modesty, self-emptiness, in being void of desires, quiet and free from exertion. Hence, his followers profess to seek virtue by abstraction from the world and the repression of desire. This latter, they suppose, is to be effected by eating their spirits or stifling their breath. The better to gain the end, they retired to the tops of mountains to commune with reason and to reach insensibility.

The term Taou, means path or way, and some understand it as denoting eternal reason. At all events, to this Laou-tze refers all things as the ultimate ideal unity of the universe. Thus he writes: "All things originate from Taou, conform to Taou, and to Taou at last return. Formless, it is the cause of form. It is an eternal road; along it all beings and all things walk; but no being made it, for it is being itself, and yet nothing, and the cause and effect of all."

He regarded the human soul as "the essence or substance of the body—a vapour which escapes at death." In like manner, he held that "the stars are divine; the five great planets being the essences of the five elements of our globe—Mercury of water; Venus of metal; Mars of fire; Jupiter of wood; and Saturn of earth." If Confucius went to one extreme, in ignoring supernatural powers, Laou-tze, or at least his followers, went to the other in the number of the spirits to which they gave reverence, and the multitude and frequency of the service rendered to them. In fact, Taouism has become, next to Hindooism and Fetichism the most materialistic, polytheistic, and thoroughly debasing, idolatrous creed in the world. It has its sea-gods and land-gods; its gods of woods, hills and rivers, of thunder and lightning, of fire and wind, and all the phenomena of nature; of all the productions of the soil; of health, of wealth and office; of each particular district, department and province of the land, with genii and inferior divinities without number, having separate spirits to take charge of each of the four corners of the house, and the shop, parlour and kitchen of every dwelling.

The Taouists profess to have intercourse with these spirits, and even to be able to bring them under their control. For this purpose, they busy themselves with fasts and sacrifices, amulets and charms, and spend much time in the study of astrology, alchemy and similar arts. The head of their priesthood is supposed to control the deities of various districts, appointing and removing them as the Emperor does his officers. In reality, the Chinese have very low ideas of these spirits. They regard them as not only inferior to the visible heavens, but as ranking below ancient sages or even modern rulers, and in this case they suppose that no tutelary divinity can exercise his function in any given district without the warrant of their chief priest. From the power which this individual possesses, his handwriting is supposed to be efficacious against all noxious influences; and charms written by him are sold at a high price. Each priest issues similar amulets, which yield a large revenue, more particularly as their efficacy only lasts for a year.

BUDDHISM.

But the working of these two systems left in the Chinese mind still a void, particularly a desire for more light on the future destiny of man. This afforded an opportunity for Buddhism, which was introduced into China, it is said, in the first century of the Christian era. But here, to accommodate itself to the Chinese mind, it gave up some of its most cherished notions. It relinquished its hostility to Theism, only giving Buddha the highest place among the gods; for Nirvana it substituted a "peaceful land in the West," presided over by another Buddha named Amitaba, or "boundless space;" for contemplation it substituted prayer; and, while holding the doctrine of transmigration of souls, and believing that the souls of their ancestors might be in any of the animals around, it yielded to the practice of eating flesh. Nothing could better illustrate the moral weakness of the system than its readiness to accommodate itself to opposite principles for the purpose of gaining adherents.

The empire is now full of Buddhist temples, and the priests swarm everywhere. They profess to renounce all family connections, take a vow of celibacy, shave their heads and abstain from animal food. They worship the three precious Buddhas—the past, the present, and the future—besides a variety of subordinate divinities, such as Kwan-yin, the goddess of mercy, the god of wealth, etc.

CHAPTER V.

RELIGIOUS OBSERVANCES AND MORAL CONDITION OF THE CHINESE.

"I perceive that in all things ye are too superstitious."—Acts xvii. 23.

OF the three religions of China, sketched in our last chapter, Confucianism is that of the learned, and is most countenanced by the Government. The works of Confucius are the class-books of the schools and the subjects of the public examinations, so that the learned pride themselves in being his followers, but the common people generally adhere to one of the other two, and the majority to Buddhism. We are not, however, to conceive of the followers of these three systems as separated into opposing sects. In general, the three faiths, if they may be so called, dwell together or are amalgamated in the Chinese mind. Sometimes the Confucian will speak with contempt of the Buddhist priests, on account of the indolence of their lives and their professions of celibacy, both so contrary to Chinese ideas. Perhaps he will also exclaim against the demonology of the Taouists, but still he joins in their worship. In fact, in the religion of the Chinese there is a blending of the three systems. Taouism and Buddhism both honour and profess to adopt the morality of Confucius, while the adherents of the latter join in the services of the others. Taouism furnishes the gods of literature and war, as well as the tutelary gods of districts and towns, while Buddhist priests must take part in all important religious observances in public, and the priests of both these systems attend the same funerals and weddings, and pray together side by side, as if their systems were identical in principle and purpose.

In considering, therefore, the religious worship of the Chinese, we do not consider it necessary to treat of their observances in relation to these distinctive systems. All that we shall attempt, therefore, is to give a short account of their leading religious practices, and then of their moral condition as a people.

SECTION I.—RELIGIOUS OBSERVANCES.

EMPEROR'S OFFICE.

At the centre of their religious services are the offerings of the Emperor in person at the altars of the temple of Heaven in Peking, the most important of these being the sacrifice and prayer offered by him at the South altar, in the open air at the winter solstice. He is the Pontifex Maximus, or Sovereign Pontiff, the people are his children, and he is the Son of Heaven. As its delegate and vicegerent, he has the right to rule over all under the skies, and he alone mediates between it and his people. On several important occasions, therefore, but particularly at the season mentioned, he with great pomp offers a burnt-offering and various other oblations to Shang-ti, or Heaven. There has been much dispute among missionaries, Catholic and Protestant, as to the meaning of this title, whether it expresses the idea of a personal ruler, or the material heaven. The majority seem now to agree that, though in its earliest use it probably had reference to the one God, it has in the Chinese religion been long expressive of the visible heaven. In fact, the Chinese do not seem to have any conception of a pure, independent spirit originating, supporting and governing all things, and attach materialistic ideas to all that they say on this subject. To Shang-ti, then, as expressive of the sky above, the Emperor renders honour as an humble servant to a superior, but to it alone. He at the same time offers services to others— to the spirit of the earth, the spirits of the sun, the moon, the grain and the land. But to them he speaks as a superior, praising them for their beneficial acts and influences. These services, plainly a remnant of their original nature-worship, is the centre of a system of idolatry which ramifies through every sphere of Chinese life.

ANCESTOR-WORSHIP.

But the most characteristic feature of Chinese religion is their ancestor-worship. This has been held up by European writers as "a harmless if not meritorious respect for the dead." Missionaries who have thoroughly examined the subject, and have had opportunities of learning its real nature, tell us that those who talk thus simply "know little about it." It is a real idolatry, not indeed in the letter, but in the spirit, the Chinese rendering their offerings to the departed in the most profoundly religious way of which their natures are capable.

The Chinese believe that each person has three spirits, or, perhaps more correctly, three forms of the one spirit essence. The one goes with the body to the grave, the second wanders like the genii on the mountains, and the third resides in the ancestral tablet, before which religious worship is devoutly paid. The practice was in existence before Confucius, but he endorsed it, probably with the view of encouraging filial piety, which he regarded as the sum of all morality, and it is now the most widely-spread religious custom in China, and the most powerful in its hold upon the mind of all classes. For each departed ancestor a tablet is erected, twelve to fifteen inches high, before which incense is burned night and morning. For a deceased father, the ceremonial must be kept up for forty-nine days. These tablets, as time rolls onward, become very numerous. A family is mentioned in Canton, having in their dwelling two rooms with 1,100 in each, and a third containing an image of their ancestor, a disciple of Confucius, who lived B.C. 300. In such rooms the tablets are arranged from above downward, commencing with the oldest. For these ancestral halls are endowed, that they may be kept in repair to the latest generations, for it is held that the honours paid to ancestors are necessary even for thousands of years.

The occasions of making offerings to the spirits of their deceased ancestors are very numerous. On the anniversaries of births and deaths in the family, at particular eras in a man's history, as when a scholar obtains a degree, or an officer an advance in rank, indeed on the occurrence of any event of family interest, but especially at the great annual feast of the tombs, the departed are honoured in this way. The objects of the offerings are, first, to provide for the comfort of the departed, and secondly, to save their descendants from their wrath, which they might incur from neglect. There is no idea of propitiating an offended god or securing his favour. Even the costly and elaborate feasts provided are intended as food for the support of the ghosts. As this remains as large as before, they suppose that the spirits partake of the flavour, while the substance remains, which serves to gratify the more gross appetites of the priests or worshippers, though the Chinese maintain that after these spirits have partaken of the more subtle portions, the rest has no more taste than the white of an egg.

Further, the Chinese suppose that the invisible world is but the image of this, and not only do the spirits need food for their support there as here, but that some ready cash is necessary to meet unavoidable expenses. Hence every pious Chinaman must remit to his deceased ancestors annually some money. This fices to these spirits, that they may obtain success in is done by taking small pieces of paper and affixing to the centre patches of tinfoil or gold leaf, representing gold and silver, and then burning them, in which act they are supposed to pass in invisible bullion to their relatives on the other side of the river. The preparation of this sacrificial paper gives employment to myriads, and it forms a large article of trade.

But besides food and money, they feel it necessary that their relatives should have clothing and other articles. Hence they delineate on paper various garments and transmit them in the same way. But in addition, some will construct houses with furniture, cooking utensils, etc., everything ready for use on arrival, draw up a proper conveyance of the whole for the benefit of their friends, have the same duly signed and sealed before witnesses, then burn it with the house, and rejoice in the assurance that their friends beyond will have comfortable and well-furnished homes, and hold them, too, by an unassailable title.

But Chinese character is seen in these services. The offerings of food consist of vegetables, rice, fruit and confectionery, piled up in baskets and basins seemingly full to overflowing, but in reality with the centres filled with coarse paper or plantain stalk, and the food thinly scattered over the top. Their excuse for this is that the spirits know no better.

In reality, however, the feature of filial piety which has given these services a respect in the eyes of many in Christian lands, is not so much the motive for them, as fear that some part of the deceased's spirit floating about should take vengeance for neglect. Those who have witnessed a household engaged in their devotions before their ancestral tablets, represent it as an occasion of almost mortal terror on the part of all engaged. So the reverence paid at the graves of ancestors is the result of a dread that the spirit may break forth and wreak vengeance.

The Buddhists have added to this the idea of a place similar to the Romish purgatory, and, like the priests of Rome, claim the sole authority to deliver from it. Hence they manage to get themselves employed at every funeral, to release the departed soul from that place, in order that it may avail itself of what has been provided for it by surviving relatives. For this purpose, of course, money is required; and it is stated that it is no uncommon thing for them to draw from the bereaved family to the amount of $1,000, to release their relative from Yung-Kan, the dark world prison, lest in time he should break out himself and wreak terrible vengeance on their persons, business, or property. These fellows also get up public services for the benefit of those wretched ghosts, which have no posterity to do it for them, for which, of course, they must have money.

The performance of these duties is one of the most solemn obligations devolving upon children throughout the empire. It may, therefore, be supposed that the amount expended in this way must be very large. Dr. Yates, of Shanghai, estimates it at the rate of six shillings sterling per family, which, allowing five for a family in four hundred millions, would give a total of $120,000,000. Besides this, at the festivals of the district, departmental and provincial deities, it is customary to make charitable offerings to the spirits of the dead poor, whose friends are not able to make the necessary provision for their comfort, or whose burial-places are unknown. The same authority estimates the amount expended on the occasion of the first two, not counting the last, as amounting to over $31,000,-000, making a total of $151,000,000—twenty times the amount contributed by all Christendom for the conversion of the heathen.

Besides these, there are a great variety of services to other spirits. As every city in this world has its superior magistrate, so it must have its superior spirit in the other world, to which all coming from it must be subject, and his temple is much frequented. The farmer holds an annual festival, at which he offers sacrifices to the spirits of the horse, the cow, and the hills. And so on, we might almost say, *ad infinitum*.

We may add here, that there are throughout the empire 1,560 temples to Confucius, and one day annually is kept sacred to his memory. On one occasion of this kind there were offered 62,600 animals, besides 27,600 pieces of silk, all provided by Government, in addition to the numerous offerings presented by private individuals.

Yet all this worship has respect only to the present life and even to its most secular affairs. The mass of the Chinese go to their temples and render their sacrifices to these spirits that they may obtain success in business or advancement in political life, and much in the same way as they offer gifts to officials to secure their favourable influence.

With the Chinese all the services either of Confucianism or Buddhism do not engage a tithe of the money or thought that ancestral worship does. Nor is it the praiseworthy or even harmless thing which some liberal Christians represent. It is a denying of the only living and true God, and changing "the glory of the incorruptible God for an image like to corruptible man." It involves a farther untruth of extensive influence, viz., that the spirits of the dead can revisit their posterity, and the gross absurdity that they can be provided with food, clothing and houses by the process of fire.

In its moral influence it is most debasing. There is something terrible to a Chinese in the idea of dying without a son to attend to his grave, or to sacrifice to his shade, and his spirit in consequence wandering hungry, naked and homeless in the under world. Hence the custom of infant marriages, which has been pronounced "a fruitful source of female degradation, misery and suicide." Farther, it fosters polygamy and its attendant evils. The desire for sons to render the sacrifices required by this system, leads men to take as many wives as they can keep, or to indulge in unrestrained concubinage. It is also one of the causes of infanticide. Female children are not desired, and their coming is reckoned a calamity, for the reason, among others, that they cannot render the required services to the parents when dead. Owing to this system also widows commit suicide that they may be accounted "virtuous and filial," and have their names inscribed on tablets placed in the temple and incense offered before them.

There is, however, one farther evil connected with it which must be particularly mentioned, as it comes home to us with practical power. It is the reason why the Chinese do not emigrate in families. They dislike to move away, because they must leave the tombs of their ancestors and cease to render the sacrifices due to them. Hence only certain male members of the family in any instance leave, and these only temporarily, expecting to return home when they have acquired a certain amount of the foreigners' money. This leads to overcrowding of their cities and other districts, with consequent poverty and wretchedness. The population is overflowing and emigration a necessity, so that they are now coming to the Australian Colonies, the Indian Archipelago, the Sandwich Islands, and particularly California and British Columbia, from which they are spreading across the continent. But the emigrants are all males, with the exception of a few ruined females, not averaging one in a hundred. Mr. Williamson, in his "Journeys in North China, Manchuria and Mongolia," says that in the two latter "there are scores of towns where there is not one respectable Chinese woman,—only communities of males, among whom the most abominable vices are perpetrated."

FUNG SHUI.

Connected with this system of ancestral worship is a modern superstition known as Fung Shui, which is peculiar to China, and occupies so important a place in all the transactions of life among her people that it is necessary to give some account of it. Still it is difficult for a foreigner to understand it, and about as difficult for him to realize the influence which it has in all the affairs of this singular race. Regard for this is universal. A Chinaman may be a Confucian, a Taouist or a Buddhist, but none of them refuse to honour Fung Shui. He may join in the services of one system at one time, and of another at another, but Fung Shui he regards at all times and at every period of life. "It is the atmosphere he breathes, under its influence he lives and dies, according to its principles he is buried, and by its laws he expects to be governed in the world to come."

What, then, is Fung Shui? It has been defined as "the science of luck." It is a mysterious principle, pervading earth, air and water, on the presence of which depends every good and evil that men enjoy or suffer here below. The word means wind-water, and is supposed to represent a remnant of their original nature-worship. At the foundation of it is the idea, that all genial influences come from the South and all harmful from the North, and that these proceed in straight lines. This perhaps originated in a view of facts in nature—that winter comes with cold winds from the North, that thus nature decays, man suffers discomfort, and, from their scarcity of clothing and fuel, disease and death then prevail. So, on the other hand, spring comes with the South wind, bringing comfort to man and reviving vegetation. The richest returns to the husbandman are received from exposure to the South, the invalid finds health in a more genial clime to the South, and even the birds of the air recognize the same influence.

This principle they apply to all the affairs of human life. Every harmful influence, whether as regards business, crops, health, family interest or political preferment, is supposed to come from the North, and everything favourable from the opposite direction. And so a great part of life is taken up, in discovering and carefully observing those measures necessary to resist the North evil upon childhood, middle life and old age, upon friendships, marriages, births, employments, contracts, voyages, construction of houses, gambling or schemes of roguery, and, perhaps above all, the location and digging of graves, while equal care is necessary in drawing forth the good influences that come from the South. The building of a house on a certain spot or to a certain height, or with the corners set in a certain position, even an extra cornice or an addition to the chimney, might turn an evil influence upon a house a mile away, or might arrest the benign arrangements of good Fung. Hence the erection of a building, or even the cutting down of a few trees, cannot be undertaken without a due consideration of the bearings of the act upon the whole neighbourhood. So in regard to success in business or in study, the maintaining of health or the birth of sons, Fung Shui is supposed to rule everything.

But not only does this influence bind the Chinaman in life; the fortunes of a family will depend upon their selection of a spot for the tombs of the parents, under the auspicious influence of this mysterious principle. Bodies remain unburied for years till such a place is found, and when it is pointed out it must be purchased at any cost.

Those only who have resided among the Chinese, can understand the extent to which this superstition pervades the whole of Chinese society. No other idea so dominates the mind of the whole nation, and to foreigners among them, its influence appears in connection with every scheme of public improvement. It has met every proposal for the construction of railways and telegraphs. These go in straight lines, thus affording facilities for every evil influence, while the telegraph poles, railway cuttings and signals would compel the good spirits to turn aside in every direction and throw everything into confusion. So the cutting through hills or opening of graves, would let loose any number of invisible spirits fully determined on vengeance. So, too, the building of bridges, the digging of canals, the working of coal mines have all come into collision with Fung Shui. And it is a trouble to all foreigners in regard to buildings, and especially to missionaries in regard to houses for themselves, or schools and churches for their work. A steeple higher than surrounding buildings may arrest some good influence or turn a bad one upon another part of a town, and hence missionary buildings have to be modified in structure, or sometimes taken down altogether. Not long since it was decided that the Fung Shui of a Chinese temple at Fuchow required that a large, well-built and long-occupied set of buildings of the English Church Missionary Society should be removed. It is even asserted that "multitudes of localities in China to-day are practically inaccessible to mission work" from this cause.

Such is a brief sketch of the religious systems and practices of this remarkable people. It will be seen that their history, instead of showing an ascent from atheism to pure conceptions of God, exhibits a descent from purer views, through less pure, to a more deeply debasing system. This accords with the Scriptural account of idolatry as an apostasy from the knowledge of the true God. In their earliest records we find the conception of one living God and personal ruler. But, "knowing God, they glorified Him not as God, neither gave thanks." Next we find them turning to nature-worship, or, as the apostle expresses it, "worshipping and serving the creature rather than the creator." "They became vain in their reasonings, their senseless heart was darkened," and they sank into the lowest polytheism. It must be admitted that their worship exhibits neither the impurity nor the cruelty to be found in the religious systems of India, but in absurdity it is unsurpassed by that of the tribes of earth deemed the lowest in intelligence. The fact is most instructive. Here is a people of no inferior intellect, who, indeed, in shrewd, practical sagacity will compare with any people on the globe, among whom education is as widespread as in some nominally Christian lands, whose statesmen have been pronounced by Sir Frederick Bruce to be "equal to any he ever met in any capital in Europe," whose merchants cope successfully with the British, and are even gaining ground upon them in the marts of the East, and whose sons in fair competition have won honours in British and American Universities, yet in things spiritual and divine exhibiting a silliness in their views and a puerility in their practices, which form one of the most impressive illustrations of the divine saying, "Professing themselves to be wise, they became fools."

SECTION II.—MORAL CONDITION.

But what of their moral condition? Does the apostle Paul's description, in Rom. i., of the low morality resulting from the disowning the true God and turning to the worship of idols, hold true in this case? Do we not find pure moral precepts in the works of Confucius, even something like the Golden Rule, and do not the Chinese show regard for them in their practice? We at once answer the last inquiries in the affirmative; but here it must be observed, that we by no means maintain that Christianity first revealed to man the moral law. The heathen everywhere show some knowledge of the right. As the apostle says

"They show the work of the law written upon their hearts." Perhaps the principles of morality are as clearly exhibited in the writings of the sages of China, as they ever were by any people without revelation. But where their teaching is defective is: 1. That their conceptions are imperfect and darkened, compared with what is enjoyed under the perfect light, which Christianity pours upon every question of duty. 2. That they want the perfect ideal of virtue in human life, which we have in the person of the incarnate Son of God. 3. That they want the moving power which there is in the love of Christ, evoking love in the hearts of His followers; and the practical result is a morality below that of Christian lands. In China there has been the fairest opportunity of testing the question. The whole people profess entire subjection to the teaching of a man, who not only aimed at morality, but who made it his religion. We may admit, too, that among its millions there are many who live tolerably decent lives, as regards the ordinary duties of life, and that on the whole their moral condition is not so debased as that of some other heathen nations. But yet the testimony of those who have had the best opportunities of becoming acquainted with their real character, is that the statement of the apostle is true of them as of others, "knowing the ordinances of God, that they which practise such things are worthy of death, they not only do the same, but also consent with them that practise them."

Mr. Williamson, while speaking of them in the

highest terms as the imperial race in the far East, adds: "It is true at present they are in a most deplorable condition. Their old principles of government are disregarded; the maxims of their classics utterly ignored by the generality of their rulers; rapacity and corruption pervade every department of the State, even to a far greater degree than foreigners ever imagined." Then he quotes at length from Chinese authority, particularly a memorial to the throne from the governor of Kiang-su, a man of great authority and position, who, describing men as obtaining office by purchase, says: *"It is known that these men, who thus receive their appointments from the Board of Revenue, can henceforth fraudulently appropriate the Government revenues, can henceforth plunder and oppress the people; in hearing a trial, can make the wrong appear the right; in the pursuit and apprehension of criminals, can cause it to be falsely testified that virtuous men are robbers."*

"This testimony," says Mr. Williamson, "is true, not of Kiang-su alone, but of the whole empire. Poverty on the part of the Government has induced them to depart from their old plan of competition and dispose of their magistracies for money. . . But the most melancholy fact is that there is about as little hope apart from these 'hungry tigers.' Superstition clouds the finest intellects, as we have repeatedly witnessed; a low and mean spirit has crept into the homes, even of the highest classes; squalor and filth are often barely concealed beneath the grand silks and embroidered dresses of the wealthy; opium is gnawing at the vitals of the empire and destroying thousands of its most promising sons. And, worst of all, *there is no truth in the country. Falsehood and chicanery are their hope and their weapons. Scheming has been reduced to a science; deceit and lying placed upon the pedestal of ability and cleverness.* The common people know not when they may be pounced upon by their own protectors; and so a paralyzing sense of insecurity pervades the country throughout its whole extent."

In another place, describing the obstacles in the way of China's progress, he says: "The last I shall refer to is the absence of truth and uprightness and honour. This is a most appalling void, and, unfortunately, it meets one in *all classes and professions of the people.* I do not refer to money matters, for, as a rule, they stand well in this respect, inasmuch as they know that unless they fulfilled their business engagements, they would soon cease to have any business at all. I refer to general matters, and for illustrations may point to every page of our intercourse with them." "Most emphatically they need something which shall *awaken moral sense, create* the *fear* of God, and *adjust* and *strengthen the conscience.*"

And as to the future, he says: "There is no hope for China in China itself. I have at different times, in different connections, inquired separately of the ablest Europeans and Americans in Peking—men who had the best opportunities of knowing the true state of matters—whether they had ever met a man in official circles, who understood the times and was likely to put forth some intelligent effort to raise his country, and the reply has invariably been in the negative." This accords with my own observation. There is not a man at present within the field of view in China of whom anything toward the reorganization and the elevation of the people can be expected. The nation, therefore, must become more and more corrupt, unless some external element be introduced to save it."*

The Chinese have indeed been regarded as benevolent. All their benevolence, however, is confined to the inferior animals. Buddhism teaches that even insects must not be killed, lest one should cause the death of some departed friends, whose souls may inhabit them. Their priests are vegetarians for the same reason, and have reservoirs of water in which they keep alive fish, snakes, tortoises, etc. They also keep in their temples a number of fat hogs and lazy dogs, till they die of obesity or scurvy. But against the cry of distress from their fellow-men, their hearts are closed. The sick poor are allowed to perish by the roadside without a helping hand. Persons in danger of being drowned or burned are seldom rescued, and the dying are turned out to die in the open air, to save the trouble of cleansing the house of their ghosts, when they are dead.

To show how ineffective is their boasted civilization or religious systems, to induce any real humanity, we

---

* Williamson's "Journeys in North China," etc.

have only to advert to the punishments inflicted under their laws. The editor of the *China Mail*, published at Hong Kong, thus describes one of them: " It means being tied to a cross, and then subjected to tortures so fiendish, that even the North American Indian has never invented anything more horrible; for the death agony is prolonged through such operations as flaying the face, cutting off the breasts, excising the muscles, nipping off the fingers and toes, and finally disembowelling the wretched victim, who even then has been known to manifest signs of life."

Farther, of the "every day" punishments in China, he says: "These are described by a well-known writer as follows: Compressing the ankles, and squeezing the fingers between boards until crushed, twisting the ears, kneeling on chains, striking the lips until jellied, putting the hands in stocks behind the back, or tying the hands to a bar under the knees, and chaining the neck to a stone. Cases are *officially* recorded of nailing prisoners' hands between boards, scalding with boiling water, inserting red-hot spikes, cutting the tendon Achilles, burying the body up to the neck in lime, while the prisoner is forced to swallow large draughts of water. Finally, a lighter (?) punishment is to make the criminal kneel on a mixture of pounded glass, sand, and salt, until the knees are excoriated. There are many other minor punishments, but we have omitted one we knew to be practised at Shanghai on some rebels, captured by the Imperialists during the Taiping rebellion, viz., driving fine spikes of bamboo down between the nails of the fingers and toes." On this occasion, the Government commander Yeh is said to have beheaded not less than 80,000 rebels. When we add that such punishments are not unfrequently inflicted for insignificant crimes, and sometimes to gratify the malice or greed of the officiating mandarin, we have surely said enough to show what a strangely callous indifference there is in the Chinese nature, in regard to the sufferings of others.

We have already referred to the prevalence of polygamy and its attendant evils, but we must particularly notice the infanticide. This is not taught by any religious system, or practised as a religious rite; but as females cannot make the offerings of food to the spirits of their deceased parents, the birth of a girl causes only lamentations, and many infants are in consequence drowned in tubs of water, strangled, or buried alive. In the great cities of the empire, thousands are yearly exposed to die, simply to avoid the trouble of rearing them. The Buddhists avail themselves of this, to fill their monasteries, by picking up the abandoned children. Others do the same from the basest motives: rearing them for gain, selling them into domestic slavery, or for base gratifications; or keeping them to beg, having first put out their eyes. It is said to be quite common to see on the streets of their cities, men with baskets slung on a pole, with female infants selling at sums of from forty cents upward. Bainbridge says that half the baby girls throughout China might be bought for a few dollars apiece, and the trade is defended, on the ground that it saves them from being put to death. Generally the household servants are slaves, many having been thus bought in infancy; and there is the concubinage common in such a state of society. Boys are sometimes sold, but they are generally bought for the purpose of adoption. But women are generally kept in the most abject slavery. Girls in a family, and wives, until they have borne a son, are a species of property and liable to be sold at the will of the husband and father, who has even the power of life and death over them.

As to grosser forms of vice, Mr. Williams (Middle Kingdom, I. 834) says: "With a general regard for outward decency, they are vile and polluted in a shocking degree; their conversation is full of filthy expressions, and their lives of impure acts." If, therefore, the influence of heathenism has been less debasing among the Chinese than among some races—if there we find the working of the natural conscience in the discharge of relative duties, as strongly as among any people without revelation, the description of the apostle is still applicable to them: "As they refused to have God in their knowledge, God gave them up unto a reprobate mind, to do those things which are not fitting."*

---

* The principal authorities for the statements in this and the previous chapter are "Medhurst's China and the Chinese," "Williamson's Journeys in North China, Manchuria, and Mongolia," "Gracey's work in the Outline Missionary Series," published by Snow and Co., and articles in the "Encyclopedia Britannica."

CHAPTER VI.

JAPAN AND HER RELIGION.

"Listen, O isles, unto me; and hearken, ye people, from far."—Isa. xlix. 1.

CIRCUMSTANCES have of late directed much attention to Japan and her people. The physical features of the country, the richness of its products, its long seclusion from intercourse with the West, its singular civil institutions and social customs, the skill in various arts shown by the people, their rapid adoption of European views and practices, and the remarkable progress which they have been making in education, science, and civilization, have all tended to invest them with peculiar interest; while their moral and social condition has touched the sympathy of the Christian Church, and drawn forth vigorous efforts from various sections of it for their evangelization. As their religious condition presents some peculiarities, a more particular account of it may be given.

Japan consists of a long chain of islands, lying off the coast of Asia, between 24° and 50° 40′ north latitude, and from 124° to 156° east longitude. It is supposed to contain an area of 148,000 square miles, or one-fourth more than the United Kingdom. Its population is over 34,000,000.

Three religious systems are found among them, Shintoism, Buddhism, and Confucianism. The first of these is the original religion of the country. The word Shinto means the way of the gods; and with the Japanese, Japan is the country of the gods. The great object of veneration under this system is the sun-goddess, but so exalted is she deemed, that she is addressed in prayer only through the mediation of inferior divinities, the large majority of which are the deified military and civil heroes, connected with the Imperial dynasty, and—what forms the distinguishing feature of their worship—through the Emperor or Mikado, who is considered her descendant and representative on earth. During a lengthened period however, the civil power was wrested from him, and he was but a puppet in the hands of the Shogun, or commander-in-chief of the army, and the Daimyos or feudatory nobles, retaining however all the time his ecclesiastical authority. But in 1868 he regained his temporal supremacy.

The Miyas, as the Shinto temples are called, are usually situated among groves of trees, and are built in very simple style, being generally of white wood without the brilliant colouring of the Buddhist temples. These are approached by a number of ornamented gateways, called *torii*. As the name implies, these were originally a single perch for the fowls offered to the gods, not as food, but to give warning of daybreak. In time they assumed the character of a general symbol of their worship, and their number became unlimited. Internally these temples are marked by the absence of decoration and the simplicity of their arrangements. The furniture usually consists of a mirror of highly polished white metal, designed to symbolize the sun, and a table or altar. In most, however, are images of the divinities to which they are dedicated; but it is said that they are not set up for worship, but kept in secret recesses, and only exhibited on particular occasions.

The forms of Shinto worship are exceedingly few and simple. On approaching the temple, the worshipper first performs his ablutions in an adjoining tank, and then strikes a bell suspended before the door, in order to arouse the attention of the resident spirit, or rather, as some conjecture, to drive away evil influences from the neighbourhood. Next he kneels in the verandah opposite a grated window, through which he fixes his eyes upon the sacred mirror, offers a short prayer, presents a sacrifice of rice, tea, fruits or the like, deposits a little money in a box, and takes his departure. Great stress is laid upon the manifestation of cheerfulness on the part of the worshipper. The temple must not be approached with a downcast spirit or a sorrowful countenance, for that might disturb the peaceful beatitude of the divinity. The money deposited goes into the purse of the priest, and the offerings of fruit to his table. In the gardens and courtyards of the Shinto worshippers, there are miniature miyas, where they perform their private devotions.

The duties inculcated by this system are principally ceremonial, such as the observance of festival days, pilgrimages to shrines, worship at home and in the temples, and abstinence from a great variety of forms of corporeal defilement. Thus the eating of the flesh of a four-footed animal, except deer, renders one unclean for thirty days. So, for a longer or shorter period, will contact with his own or another person's blood, associating with an impure person, killing a beast, attending a dying person, or entering a house where a dead body is lying. In the more serious cases, the impurity can be removed only by a long course of purification, through fasting, prayer, and the solitary study of devotional books.

But the most sanctifying ceremony of Shintoism, is the pilgrimages to the sacred shrines, of which there are twenty-two through the empire; the most honoured of which is an ancient temple of the sun-goddess at Tsye, at which she is said to have been born and reared. At these places, the devotee, on the payment of a small sum of money to the priest, obtains a voucher or *ofarria*, which is a scrap of paper, with a few Japanese characters on it. It is a kind of absolution or remission of sins, but it is believed to secure health, prosperity, and children in this world, and a happy future beyond death. Those who cannot visit these shrines in person, send for an *ofarria*, which can be obtained for money; but the zealous aim at making such a pilgrimage at least once a year.

There is no moral code connected with their worship.

In fact their most renowned writer, in a commentary on their most venerated writings, asserts that in Japan there is no need of any system of morals, as every Japanese acted aright, if he only consulted his own heart.

Buddhism was introduced into Japan some five centuries after the Christian era, and spread extensively, many welcoming its dreary light on the future, in contrast with the darkness of the old system. Previously to the revolution of 1868, it received the support of Government, but on the restoration of the Mikado to power, that has been withdrawn. Confucianism again has been adopted by the learned, who studied the Confucian classics, as foreign oracles of wisdom, but it has few temples.

The latest accounts, however, represent the popular faith in all these ancient creeds as thoroughly unsettled. The attendance upon either the Buddhist or Shinto temples is generally small. Among the causes of this are the introduction of Western ideas and the spread of education. Japan has now 25,000 schools, with an average daily attendance of 1,500,000 pupils, with high schools having 20,000 scholars in attendance, and two Universities, giving very advanced and thorough training, the one with 800 students, the other with about half as many. The alarming fact, however, is that in breaking loose from their old religious ties, multitudes, particularly of the educated classes, are relapsing into avowed infidelity.

In regard to the moral condition of this people, it

will be sufficient to give a single extract from a letter of one of the missionaries labouring among them. The Rev. S. G. McLaren, of the United Presbyterian Church of Scotland, thus writes:—

"The really great progress which Japan has made of recent years has challenged the attention of the whole world. With a rapidity almost miraculous, she has assumed the features of modern civilization, and it is apt to be taken for granted that the character and morals of her people have advanced in the same rapid ratio. This conclusion has been fostered by many modern travellers, who have described the Japanese in terms of the most extravagant praise. They are represented as not only frank and joyous in their disposition, simple and unsophisticated in their habits, but as pure and spotless in their morals, and as living in a state of almost primeval innocency. Now this is utterly misleading, and quite inconsistent with fact. It grieves me to say a single word which may tend to degrade the people and the country to which I have given my life, but truth compels me to say that on the whole they are a depraved and licentious people. None know this better, and none mourn it more, than the better class of Japanese themselves. It is not in the cities alone that immorality prevails. In some of the rural districts the marriage bond is almost nominal, and the state of morals loose beyond description. An American physician in Yokohama, who has resided long in the country, who has practised in the Japanese Government hospitals, and who knows the people well, estimates that *about two-thirds of the whole population are suffering from diseases, hereditary or acquired, which are the direct consequences of immoral living.* Our own medical agent, Dr. Fauld, believes this is an extreme estimate, and that the experience on which it is based must be exceptional; but in the course of his own large practice, he has had abundant and painful experience of the wide prevalence of such diseases. Dr. Hepburn, the senior missionary in Japan, who has practised in China and America, as well as in Japan, says that the state of matters here is worse than in China, and immeasurably worse than in the lowest parts of New York.

"The Japanese are not fond of dwelling on the blots on their country, but occasionally an article appears in the native papers, which reveals the deep degradation of the people. There cannot be a doubt that licentious habits are sapping the vital energies and weakening the stamina of her people." We may add, that it is asserted that but few of them pass the age of forty years.

CHAPTER VII.

AFRICA, HER PEOPLE AND HER RELIGIONS.

"Their sorrows shall be multiplied, that hasten after another God : THEIR DRINK OFFERINGS OF BLOOD will I not offer, nor take up their names into my lips."—Psalm xvi. 4.

SECTION I.—COUNTRY AND PEOPLE.

WE now turn from the consideration of the moral and religious condition of those heathen people, possessed of culture and civilization, to consider the state of those still in barbarism. And first we turn to Africa, fitly known as the Dark Continent—dark because presenting large regions hitherto so utterly unknown, and dark especially on account of the low intellectual and moral state of its inhabitants. This continent is about 5,000 miles in length, and nearly as many in breadth. It covers an area of 11,000,000 square miles, and has more habitable land than either Asia or North America. Its population is estimated at 200,000,000, but there is much uncertainty as to their real numbers. The northern parts are occupied chiefly by Mohammedans, supposed to number about 50,000,000. If we reckon the Jews and Christians at 5,000,000 more, there will remain 145,000,000 of heathen.

If a line be drawn from the mouth of the Senegal, on the west coast, eastward to the Red Sea, the whole land to the south of it, with the exception of European settlements on the coast, will exhibit a mass of heathenism of the lowest kind. Of the races inhabiting this region, the Hottentots and the Bosjesmen near the Cape of Good Hope, probably, and the inhabitants of Madagascar, certainly are of the Malay race, with perhaps some admixture of the Arabic or Negro. The rest of this vast territory is inhabited by hundreds, perhaps we might say thousands, of petty tribes, belonging to what some regard as two great races; the one to the south, of which the Kafirs and the Zulus are examples, and which are classified as Bantus; the other, of various tribes across the centre of the continent, of the well-known negro type. But philologists maintain that among the apparently disconnected languages of these various tribes, there is such similarity at the foundation as shows their common origin. On this ground, as also on account of physical resemblances, some ethnologists regard them as of the same stock. Upon this question we need not enter. Whether they are two distinct races, or two branches of one, is immaterial to our present purpose. If there are resemblances, there are very important differences between them, so that it will be proper to regard them separately.

SECTION II.—THE BANTU TRIBES.

The Kafirs and kindred tribes occupy the southern portion of the continent, as far north as the 6th degree of north latitude, a territory containing 2,500,000 square miles, or almost twice as much as India, with a climate which has been pronounced the best in the world for the promotion of both animal and vegetable life. Beside Kafirs and Zulus, the tribes best known to Europeans, there are large numbers of other tribes belonging to the same stock, so that the Bantus are supposed to number 21,000,000 of souls. They are a very large race, being tall and well-made, and in size ranking next to the Polynesians and Patagonians. They possess very strong muscular frames, acute senses, and great power of endurance. They are mostly dark-skinned; a few, indeed, are comparatively fair; but, generally, they are of a clear brown complexion, and some are full black. They differ much in appearance from the negroes, their skulls being high and long. Their hair is woolly, but differs in different tribes, as to its length and quality.

Besides war and hunting, their chief employment is cattle raising. They have large herds, oxen being their most valued possession; the care of them, even the milking of the cows, devolving on the men. But some tribes inhabit towns of some size, with well-built houses, and many cultivate the ground carefully.

The tribes nearest the British colonies in South Africa, have become well known; and, judging by these, they must be described as mentally acute and logical, arguing well and keenly. In all their social and political affairs, they show much tact and intelligence. They have shown themselves capable of being organized into large law-abiding communities. Hence at various times powerful chiefs, such as Sebituane, Kreli, and Cetewayo, have formed military states, reducing neighbouring tribes to subjection, though these do not generally hold together longer than during the life-time of such leaders. They are remarkably brave and warlike. In the seven or eight wars that England has had with them, they have shown remarkable courage, even when having only the native spear and shield, to oppose to the deadly rifles of European soldiers, causing much loss of life and treasure; and, more recently, they have proved to the world their capacity on the field of Sandlhwana.

SOCIAL CONDITION.

Wars, not for territory, but for slaves, are common among the races in the interior, but not to the same extent as among the negro races farther north. The evils of this practice we shall notice when we come to speak of them. But the Kafirs proper will never be made slaves.

They practise polygamy, and purchase their wives for cattle. The women do most of the hard out-door work—planting and hoeing, grinding corn, and building their huts. But, although apparently slaves and drudges, they hold their position with great tenacity;

and from their indispensable services, and the price they bring when given in marriage, they are held in greater esteem, and have more influence than might be supposed.

As to religion, they have generally been represented as without any knowledge of a Supreme Being. They have never developed any mythology, they have neither idols nor priests, scarcely sacrifices, and they have justly been regarded as the most materialistic of heathen people. But Rowley, in his work on the "Religion of the Africans," has shown, from his own enquiries and the testimony of others, that there is a belief in an uncreated Supreme Spiritual Being, though somewhat confused and of scarcely any practical influence. "They do not regard Him as the Creator, the Preserver, and the Ruler of all things. They do not credit Him with the attributes of justice, holiness, and love. In so far as they have the power to appreciate goodness, they look upon Him as good, as gifted with power to influence the forces of nature; and as willing, under certain circumstances, to exercise it in their behalf. Except on rare occasions they do not worship or honour Him in any way. 'God is good,' say they, 'and will do well, let us honour Him or not.' Nevertheless, in seasons of great distress, they will sometimes invoke His aid." Of this he mentions instances that came under his own observation.

Of Demonolatry, or the worship of beings intermediate between deity and humanity, a system common among savages, and among none more than among the races in Central and Western Africa, there is scarcely a trace among the Zulus or the Bantu tribes best known. But they have a sort of ancestor worship. Of heaven or hell, or of rewards and punishments in a future life, they seem to have no idea, except as they have acquired it from intercourse with foreign races. They do indeed implicitly believe in existence after death, but it is simply a continuance of the present state of things, kings being kings, and slaves remaining slaves; with all the passions, caprices, and weaknesses of mortality. These spirits are supposed to have even greater power than in the days of their flesh, and are regarded as both able and willing to wreak vengeance on those who do not minister to their wants and enjoyments. Hence they pay great deference to the spirits of their immediate ancestors, invoking their aid in times of adversity, and seeking to gratify them by such offerings as they suppose will be most pleasing.

Though these tribes, however, have so little of religious worship, they have numerous superstitions, and are much under the influence of a belief in witchcraft and sorcery. As a missionary remarks, "Not a buzzard utters its low dismal cry, not a dog bays at the moon, not a bullock falls a victim to pleuro-pneumonia, not an infant dies, or a strong man succumbs to some fatal disease, but some evil-disposed person is denounced as at work destroying his fellows." The same writer thus describes life in a polygamist Kafir village, and the manner in which superstition of this kind rules all their transactions:

"The dull monotony is varied by the visit of some chief on a begging expedition, a marriage festival, the slaughter of a fat bullock for its hide, a beer party in honour of a chief or influential neighbour, the *intonjane* dance, obscene in all its aspects—a death, a hunt, an ox racing, the presence of a sacred man to offer sacrifice on the serious illness of a member of the family, or mortality among the cattle; the dance of the youths in their transition from boyhood to manhood, and by the nocturnal revelries in the largest hut, where each man, singly and in turn, dances to the lusty clapping of hands, and the most barbarous and obscene songs of an enraptured audience. Superstition pervades almost every act of this large family. An infant sleeping soundly on its mother's back, and taken across the stream for the first time, must needs have its forehead smeared with wet clay taken from the water's edge, to propitiate the mermaids that gambol in its sedgy pools. None expectorates without obliterating the expectoration. If one is prostrated by disease, the hair of a sacred cow is plaited, and tied about his neck. When an owl utters its doleful wail, it is supposed to be out on an errand of destruction for its owner. Not a buzzard approaches with solemn step, but is bringing poverty along with it. Each is jealous of, and seems secretly bent on impoverishing his neighbbour. Each suspects the other of possessing deadly charms, or of being in league with a miniature elephant, wolf, or baboon, which, amid the darkness of night, fulfils its deadly commission. On his person and in his tobacco pouch, he carries secret charms to ward off evil. When at work or on his travels, he secretly utters ejaculations to the unseen spirits, to befriend him in his hour of need." *

Hence, there has naturally arisen the witch-doctor or medicine-man, who exercises his power over them in cruel oppression. The evil influence of these men, will appear from the following extract of a letter from a missionary, written in 1870:

"There are very serious occurrences taking place in this tribe at present. Two men have lost their lives, because, as alleged by a witch-doctor, they have bewitched Kreli's cattle with lung sickness. Others are named as concerned in this destruction of the chief's cattle. I am sadly grieved. This land is being ruined by the baneful influence of the witch-doctors. Human beings, yearly, and in no small numbers, are secretly put to death through the instigation of these doctors. We hear of some after they have been despatched; and of others we never hear. This sacrifice of human life is kept a profound secret from those who are known to be hostile to the wholesale destruction to their fellow-men. There is no security for the most precious life among the people. They are all sheep for the slaughter. The butcher of a witch-doctor has only to point out his victim, where and when he likes."

A remarkable instance of the power of these men,

---

* Life of Tiyo Soga, by Rev. J. A. Chalmers.

and the credulity of the people, occurred in 1856, when one of them persuaded whole tribes to kill all their cattle, to destroy all their corn, and leave their land uncultivated, on the promise that all the animals slain, with all the Kafirs who had ever died would rise from the dead; that the earth would yield spontaneously the richest grain, and that the choicest English cattle, with abundance of guns and ammunition, would be at the disposal of every believer; moreover, that the living Kafir would also die and soon rise again, and the old resume the bloom of youth. Though, to a Kafir, his cattle are dearer than friend or family, yet it was estimated that 150,000 cattle perished under this delusion. The result was, as might be expected, a famine, in which 20,000 of the people died, and 30,000 more were scattered among the English settlements.

MORALITY.

In regard to their morality, it must be said that some tribes were found, before they had much intercourse with the whites, to be remarkably truthful and honest. But since they have lived in closer contact with them, they have become suspicious, thievish, and revengeful, the result, in a large measure at least, of the injustice with which they have been treated, their lands often being taken from them on the most flimsy pretexts. But of the tribes on the Zambesi, Dr. Emil Holub, an Austrian explorer, says that "their dishonesty is thoroughly ingrained." He also mentions among their customs the drowning the infirm and destitute; poisoning and burning on mere suspicion. He also says: "In addition to their other disgusting qualities, all the Makololos south of the Zambesi are indescribably dirty. With the exception of those who have been in service under white men, I believe the majority of them have not washed for years."* It must be added that their ceremonies and dances are gross and obscene: "chastity is unknown among them, and licentiousness is considered no disgrace to either sex."

SECTION III.—THE NEGRO RACE.

To the North of the country occupied by the Bantu tribes, lies the vast region extending across the whole continent from East to West, and Northward to the great desert of Sahara, at about latitude 20° N., inhabited by the proper Negro race. This portion of Africa is still in a great measure unexplored by Europeans; but South of latitude 15°N. it is known to possess the aspect of a connected mass of elevated land, comprising extensive table-lands, as well as high mountain groups and chains, with a vast network of rivers and lakes, the latter rivalling, if they do not excel, those of North America; and some of the former ranking with the great rivers of the earth. Here are found the richest soil, with excessively rank vegetation, dense tropical forests, with rich pastoral districts passing into the dry rainless zones of the Sahara on the North and the Kalahari desert to the South. The

---

* Quoted by Bainbridge.

West coast, which is best known, is generally low, and often a dead level for thirty or forty miles inland, with a climate rendered most pestilential by the muddy creeks and inlets, the malarious swamps, and the mangrove jungles. The rivers being barred at their mouths, or having rapids at no great distance up stream, do not afford the facilities for intercourse with the interior, which might be expected from their size. This is one reason why the countries there are so little known.

This region is inhabited by hundreds of tribes belonging to what may be called the Ethiopic or proper Negro race. But some differ very materially from that type. The Gallas, for example, to the South of Abyssinia, have a straight head, instead of the receding forehead of the pure Negro; their hair, though strongly frizzled, is not so woolly, nor are their lips so thick. Dr. Livingstone describes some whom he met on his last journey as "a fine, tall, handsome race, superior alike to the slaves seen at Zanzibar and the typical Negro of the West coast, exceedingly numerous and living in a primitive condition, utterly ignorant of the outer world."

The population of this vast region cannot be ascertained with anything like accuracy, but it is supposed to number 120,000,000. These are not only in heathen darkness, but in such a degraded condition morally and mentally, as is exhibited by few of the human family. So far as known, they exhibit a succession of petty tribes or independent kingdoms, often at war with one another. Some of them are more powerful; and those in the interior of Guinea coast, such as Ashantee, Dahomey, and others, are becoming better known. Of these, Ashantee is the most powerful, Coomassie, its capital, having a population of 100,000 souls. In some of these the people show some skill in various manufactures, and are more intelligent than we generally find the race.

Through all this region, the most marked and deplorable feature in the social condition of the inhabitants is the slave-trade, which has been carried on for centuries, by which, as Sir T. F. Buxton has said, "the whole of that immense continent has been turned into a field of warfare—a wilderness in which the people were tigers to each other." This, though not of foreign origin, has been largely promoted by the cupidity of European and Transatlantic, so-called Christian, nations. Since the discovery of America, the crimes, misery, and woe occasioned by the slave-trade across the Atlantic, no tongue can tell. It has been calculated that during three and a half centuries the number of persons shipped must have amounted to forty millions, while those who perished would probably amount to double that number. From this cause wars, cruel and incessant, have been the rule through all Negroland for ages.

Great have been the efforts made, particularly by Great Britain, to terminate this traffic, but they have not been entirely successful. As late as 1840, it was calculated that 200,000 were shipped to foreign countries, involving a sacrifice of life of double that number. Though the trade has diminished since that time, it is still carried on to some extent, while the internal traffic is still in full vigour; and, as Dr. Livingstone says, "to exaggerate its enormities is a simple impossibility." Kidnapping is carried on everywhere. Plundering expeditions between different petty tribes or larger kingdoms are frequent. Kings and chiefs sell any man in their dominions that they dislike or hate. Their own wives and children, if they survive the slaughter on the occasion of their death, are sold by their successors. Every infringement of the "customs" of the land, renders a man liable to be sold or even slain at the will of an arbitrary despot.

The evil spirit of the system pervades all society. The poor and orphans are harassed with debts and charges, which they are unable to pay, and are sold as slaves. A man inveigles his brother's children to his house, and sells them. The other says nothing, and only watches his opportunity to retaliate in kind. Such cases show how all society is poisoned by the infamous traffic, independently of the inhumanities connected with the transit of its victims from place to place, in which numbers perish.

Apart from the traffic, however, the existing slavery is an element of fearful evil. In many districts the slaves are said to be from three to ten times more numerous than the masters, and generally every other man is a slave. These have no rights. "Slave be nothing," was the language of a petty king to a missionary. Their lives are at the disposal of their master and they are slain at his will.

RELIGIOUS IDEAS.

In their religious ideas, they exhibit in its most unmixed state that form of heathenism known as Fetichism. This term is derived from the word "Fetich," first applied by Portuguese sailors to the objects of worship of the savages on the West coast, from their resemblance to the charms and talismans used by themselves, as well as by sailors of other nations. The system is defined as a belief in a peculiar power possessed by various natural objects, which is tested by experiment. In most cases, however, it will be found that the fetich worshipper has some idea of a spirit, connected with the object of his veneration. Hence the system has again been defined to be, "the doctrine of spirits, embodied in or attached to, or conveying influence through, certain material objects." Under this system homage is rendered to objects of any kind, natural and artificial—to stones, twigs, pieces of bark, roots, corn, claws of birds, teeth, skins, human or animal remains—to anything that strikes the mind of the savage as peculiar—to his hoe or other implements—to whole species of animals—to the sea and the rivers—the moon or the sun. If he fails in an undertaking, he abuses his fetich, perhaps loses faith in it, and then takes some other object on trial. Objects of this nature are seen wherever one goes in this land; "at every cross-road or ford, at every large rock or tree, at the entrance of every village, over the door of every house, and around the neck of every person he meets."

If among any people the worship is paid to the fetich itself, it is among the negroes of Africa; yet there seems little doubt that, except among the more besotted of them, there is in all their services a reference to something beyond the material object of their devotion. Many probably have only an idea of some occult mysterious power exercised in connection with it. But all the older explorers in Africa represented the inhabitants as having a belief in a supreme God, to whom they paid no worship, and by regard to whom they were but little influenced. Certain it is, that no people have been found on the earth more under the influence of a belief in demons, or spirits intermediate between God and man. "The Africans," says Rowley, "believe in the existence of God without anxiety, because they think that He is unlikely to do them harm, or to interfere in their affairs in any way; but they regard the world of spirits, by whom they believe themselves to be surrounded, with great anxiety, for they consider them to be evil rather than good; to have both the will and the power to influence and determine their destinies; and they strive, therefore, to propitiate them, or to guard themselves against their malignity. To their imagination, these spirits people the darkness with hideous shapes, poison the light with their presence, sweep over the plains in the forms of wild beasts, fill the forests, inhabit trees, live on the tops of the mountains, and in the secluded recesses of caves and valleys; make their homes in the sea, the lakes, and the rivers. The air is full of them, the earth teems with them, fire is not free from their presence, and human beings are possessed by them. To them also they attribute the sorrows and the sufferings, the misfortunes, and, in most cases, the death of mankind. But although their belief in this portion of the spiritual world, comprises almost every element found in the most elaborated systems of mythology, it is a crude, repulsive, fearful thing. No practical imagination glorifies it, and, save in some of the Western regions, it does not find an outward expression even in idolatry.'

As instances of their worship of such beings, Mr. Waddell, missionary at Calabar, mentions that among the people there, on certain occasions, a human being was sacrificed to some river or sea-god, to hasten the arrival of the ships; and that fishing villages near the mouth of the river annually devoted a man to promote their business, by bringing fish to their nets. He was tied to a stake in the river at low water, and left to be drowned by the rising tide, or devoured by alligators.

In connection with this demonolatry, faith in a system of witchcraft of various kinds is universal. Sickness and death are universally attributed to this cause. No doubt such arts are practised, with a view to the inducing of such evil consequences. One form was long known in the West Indies as the Obea. In this the individual, desirous to do the other any injury, placed the object, through which he expected to convey the malign influence, in the garden or house of the latter, believing that thus he would sicken, or waste away and die. Of such influence negroes stand in mortal terror, and some actually die from imaginary fears. From the prevalence of such views, when any person dies, or even is sick, suspicion is excited as to who is exercising the evil influence, and often it falls upon the nearest relatives. To free themselves of such suspicions they are often required to pass the ordeal of drinking poison. If the stomach of the suspected happen to be in a state that it throws this off, he is judged innocent; but the majority die under the test. On the death of a leading man at Calabar, fifty persons were obliged to undego this ordeal, of whom forty died.

To obtain recovery from sickness, or to guard against any evil that might be caused by witchcraft, as well as to obtain success in trade, or any other object desired, they have charms prepared by witch-doctors. Various objects are. employed in this way ; a human skull, heads of deer, goats or alligators, the land turtle hung up on a sacred bush, etc. "In every house but one in Creektown," we suppose that was the mission-house, Mr. Waddell "found the skulls of enemies at the doorstep, with a view of keeping out enemies." Again, in visiting the house of a leading chief, he says: "At his door were sticks set up with dead chickens, land turtle, and other things as charms. Human skulls formed the step at his door, and were seen in every corner of his yard." Indeed, it is asserted, that wars are often made solely to obtain skulls to pave the courtyard and adorn the walls of the palace.

As to the future, their views are most obscure; but nowhere does the cruelty of heathenism appear more conspicuously than in the slaughters made on the death of persons of any standing, a practice found in every part of Negro-land that has been explored. Every freeman expects to have slaves slain, to keep him company at his death, the number being determined according to his rank and wealth, and this is done mainly with the idea that this will give him importance as he enters the other world, just as the greatness of a chief's retinue does in this. Mr. Waddell mentions an instance of a hundred being killed in one day, on the death of a man of some rank. And on the death of chiefs or kings, the number would be much greater, and the slaughter not confined to slaves. He mentions the case of a petty ruler, at whose death two hundred free persons, besides slaves innumerable, were killed, part of these, however, by his orders before death or by his successor, from fear of their rivalry. Mr. W. thus describes the scene on the death of one of their petty kings named Eyamba:

"His death diffused terror through the town, yet no one dared to say that he was dead. The slaves fled in all directions. His brothers and nephew, with trusty attendants, proceeded to search the houses and immolate whom they could find. Entering a yard, they cried to their followers, 'Shut the gate, and if any escape see ye to it,' and then strangled its inmates. Armed men guarded the paths leading from the town, that none might escape to the farms and give the alarm; while others were despatched thither to seize or slay whom they could find, by road or river, in house or field.

"For the king's interment a great pit was dug, wide and deep, inside a house, and at one side of it a chamber was excavated, in which were placed two sofas. On these the body was laid, dressed in its ornaments, and a crown on its head. Then his umbrella, sword, and snuff-box bearers, and other personal attendants, were suddenly killed and thrown in with the insignia of their offices; and living virgins also, it was said, according to an old custom.

"Eyamba had many wives of the best families in the country, as also many slave concubines. He was not particular, it was said, in helping himself to whom he liked. Of the former, thirty died the first day. How many by the poison ordeal, under imputation of witchcraft against his life, we never knew. Those who were honoured to accompany him into *Obio Ekpa*, or ghostland, were summoned in succession by the message, once an honour, now a terror, 'King calls you.' The doomed one quickly adorned herself, drank off a mug of rum, and followed the messenger. Immediately she was in the hands of executioners, who strangled her with a silk handkerchief.

"Every night the work of death went on in the river, and the screams of the victims were heard both in the ships and the mission-house. Some were sent out bound in canoes and deliberately drowned. Others, returning from distant markets, chanting their paddle song, and glad to get home, but ignorant of what had taken place, were waylaid, knocked on the head, and tumbled into the river. Corpses and trunks were seen daily floating down and up with the tide, till the vessels' crews were sickened, and had to fire into them to sink them. Armed ruffians lurked in the bush by the paths, to shoot or cut down whom they could: old or young, male or female. Of the slaughters committed in the farms, only imperfect accounts were obtained, for they were carefully concealed from white people. For a time it was a reign of terror."

All the kingdoms in the section of country in which Mr. W. laboured were very small, consisting generally of a single town and some adjacent territory, not larger than a Canadian county. But in the larger kingdoms of Ashantee, Dahomey, etc., the number slaughtered on such customs is proportionally great, numbering even thousands.

On a visit to Bonny, Mr. W. describes a sacred house, known as a Jujee, or a devil-house, visited by him. "It was a horrid place, half-filled with human skulls and other unsightly objects. A pyramid of them reached from the ground to the roof. Some were old and black, others were recently cleaned; all were daubed with yellow or red paint round the eye sockets, which made them look hideous. On a platform ten feet square were several layers of them, the commencement of a new pile. There were many hundreds or thousands in that house of abominations. On another frame-work outside were fragments of human bodies, relics of a cannibal feast, made only a year or two previously, on the death of Peppel's father." He mentions at another place that, at the feast referred to, Peppel, who had been regarded as having a hand in his father's death, sent to make an attack on an unsuspecting village at a distance, where boys and girls were captured to form the delicacies of the occasion.

This leads us to notice one of the horrors of Africa, which has been frequently overlooked, viz., the prevalence of cannibalism. Though the slave-trade, rendering it more profitable to sell men than to eat them, diminished the practice, it did not extinguish it. And now the investigations of the latest travellers have shown that it exists to a horrible extent, both in the interior and near the coast. Dr. Schweinfurth describes different tribes as systematic cannibals. "One, the Niam-Niam," he says, "made no secret of their savage craving, ostentatiously stringing the teeth of their victims round their necks, adorning the stakes erected beside their dwelling, for the exhibition of their trophies, with the skulls of the men whom they have devoured."

Another, "the Monbuttoos," he says, "are a noble race,—men who display a certain national pride, and are endowed with an intellect and judgment such as few nations of the African wilderness can boast."

But yet, he adds, that "their cannibalism is the most pronounced of all the known nations of Africa. Surrounded as they are by a number of people who are blacker than themselves, and who, being inferior to them in culture, are consequently held in great contempt, they have just the opportunity which they want for carrying on expeditions of war or plunder, which result in the acquisition of a booty which is specially coveted by them, consisting of human flesh. The carcases of all who fall in battle are distributed upon the battle-field, and are prepared by drying for transport to the homes of the conquerors. They drive their prisoners before them. without remorse, as butchers would drive sheep to the shambles, and these are only reserved to fall victims on a later day to their sickening greediness."

During his stay among them, though they endeavoured to conceal the practice, yet he had ocular demonstration of its existence, on one occasion coming upon some young women engaged in preparing a human body for food by scalding the hairs off it, as he had seen done with hogs in his native land. And he was informed that almost every day during his residence a little child was killed to supply the table of the chief.

Similar details are given by Du Chaillu regarding the tribes near the West coast.

It will be seen that in all the religious views and practices above described, there is no reference to God, sin, holiness, or a future judgment. The human sacrifices have at their basis the natural instinct terribly perverted, of respect for deceased friends; but every other service among them that has the name or appearance of religion, manifests simply a selfish regard to their success or comfort in the present life.

As to their morality, after what we have said, little need be added. On this subject we are ready to welcome any blinks of natural light appearing in the darkness of heathenism. But in regard to the Negroes in Africa in their present condition, little favourable can be said. When we mention that among the tribes in Guinea the young are taught to respect the aged—that among others there is a fervid affection for the mother, though in their polygamous households, little for the father; and that under proper treatment many show a kindliness of disposition, which, under the influence of Christianity, promises well for the manifestation of Christian virtues, we have said about all that can be said in their favour. The Rev. Mr. Wilson, who gives all prominence to these traits, at the same time says, " Falsehood is universal, chastity is an idea for which they have no word," and after enumerating almost every kind of evil practice, adds, " It is almost impossible to say what vice is pre-eminent." He wrote from his knowledge of the West coast; but Capt. Burton attributes to those on the East, " every variety of vice, depravity, and mental and moral degradation, without one redeeming feature."

In the language of the missionary, from whose account of Calabar customs we have quoted, " At this day the Negro race stands before the world in a condition disgraceful to itself and to humanity. Divided into innumerable tribes and languages—without literature, laws or government, arts or sciences,—with slavery for its normal social condition, and the basest and bloodiest superstition in the world for religion—a religion without reference to God or their souls, to sin or holiness, to heaven or hell, and even without the outward insignia of temple, priest, or altar,—it has sunk so low as to be regardless alike of conscience and of shame, to reckon a man's life at his market value as a beast of burden, and to practise cannibalism, not from want but revenge, and a horrid lust of human flesh."

SECTION IV.—MADAGASCAR.

We must not, however, leave Africa without particularly noticing the island of Madagascar, which, though geographically belonging to that continent, is yet so distinct from it in her people and history.

This is the third largest island in the world, being about 1,000 miles long by 250 wide. It contains an area of 230,000 square miles, being four times that of England and Wales. It contains a population of four and a half, or some think five millions. They are, with slight admixture, of the Malay race, the same that inhabits South-Eastern Asia, and the islands of the Indian Ocean and Eastern Polynesia. Even before the introduction of Christianity, they were comparatively advanced in civilization; some being skilful in metal work, and others in spinning and weaving silk, as well as vegetable fibres, such as cotton and hemp. Many lived in towns which were skilfully fortified; the capital, Antananarivo, which is much the largest, having a population, it is supposed, of 100,000.

They have considerable mental ability. They are described as "very courageous and capable of much strenuous exertion for a short period, they are affectionate and firm in their friendships, kind to their children and to their aged and sick relatives, very respectful to old age, law-obeying and loyal, very courteous and polite, and most hospitable to strangers," but, at the same time, very immoral and untruthful, regardless of human life and suffering, and cruel in war. Drunkenness is very prevalent in most parts of the island; and of few of the tribes can it be said that they are industrious."[*]

They have no recognized system of idolatry. They have no temples, no shrines, or idols set up for worship. Their religion is a system of charm or fetich worship, in which confidence is placed in a variety of objects, to protect them from evil, or to bring special blessings. Some of these are worn on the person, and others are stones or rocks set up in prominent places. Some of these belong to individuals, but the power of others is considered so much greater that they serve as protectors for families, villages or tribes. And within a comparatively recent period there has been a special development of idolatry in one quarter, where

---

[*] Sibree in "Snow's Outline Missionary Series."

their fetiches were of such reputed power that they have been elevated to the rank of national protectors. Ancestor worship, too, has a strong hold upon them. They believe their departed friends to have become divine, in a certain sense, and they invoke their protection, offering prayers and sacrifices to them. They have also a strong belief in divination and witchcraft.

But they have never entirely lost the knowledge of the one supreme and benevolent Creator. They have such titles for him as the "Creating Prince," or "Creator." They invoke him in all their public proceedings, though in conjunction with the spirits of their deceased chiefs, but they have other titles for him, which have come down to them in proverbial sayings, which involve exalted views of his attributes and character. In them he appears as the protector of the helpless, the avenger of evil, awarder of good, the God answering prayer, the Omniscient, etc. Though this knowledge has been overlaid by superstition, and has not preserved the purer morality which appears in these proverbial sayings, yet the Malagasy have never sunk into the low religious condition of many barbarous tribes, while the missionaries find in these sayings a basis for instructing them in the knowledge of the living and the true God.

CHAPTER VIII.

POLYNESIA.

"The dark places of the earth are full of the habitations of cruelty."—Psalm lxxiv. 20.

THE Pacific Ocean is the largest in the world. But its chief interest lies in the numerous islands that stud its surface. The almost paradisaical beauty of their scenery, the richness of their soil, the variety and value of their productions, the perpetual summer of their climate, with the novel appearance, the simple life and strange habits of their inhabitants, have ever since their discovery excited the attention of the civilized world. And from the time that the modern missionary enterprise commenced, their moral and religious condition has touched the heart of the Christian Church, and awakened intense sympathy on their behalf, so that they occupy a prominent place in the history of missions.

SECTION I.—EASTERN POLYNESIA.

These islands are arranged in two great divisions, known as Eastern and Western Polynesia. These are not only distinguished by their geographical position but are occupied by races differing widely in physical conformation, colour, and language. The only exception to this is New Zealand, which by location is connected with the Western Islands, but is found inhabited by the same race that occupies the Eastern. These are allied to the Malay race, and probably originally migrated from the Indian Archipelago. The most recent study of them separates them into two divisions. The one, named the Sawiori, occupies all the groups from the Ellice Islands to the Marquesas, including the Samoas or Navigators, the Tonga and the Society Islands; also the Hawaiian group in the North Pacific, and New Zealand in the South. These are very large men, perhaps the largest in the world, in some groups averaging five feet ten inches in height. They are of a light copper colour, have straight, glossy black hair, with a Malay countenance, the nose being more flattened, and the cheek bones more prominent than in the Caucasian race. These people carried with them some culture. Though their language was not written till missionaries went among them, yet they had preserved oral traditions of their history in poems of some length. The other division, called the Tarapons, is found in the Caroline, Marshall, and Gilbert groups. They are smaller in size than the others, are generally more savage, and show less politeness in their manners, but in other respects they give indications of belonging to the same original stock. Throughout all these islands, from the Sandwich Islands to New Zealand, and away Westward in Madagascar, the languages spoken are but variations or dialects of one original tongue.

The religious ideas and moral condition of all these Islanders, before their conversion to Christianity, were much the same. They could not be considered the grossest idolaters. They had stones and other objects which they deemed sacred, or they made grotesque and repulsive wooden figures, which they set up in their temples, and before which they paid their devotions. If in this respect their worship seemed to correspond with fetichism, yet generally they professed to render their services to the spirit supposed to make the object its shrine. In general they believed in one god superior to the others, though far from partaking of the attributes of Jehovah; but they all acknowledged a multitude of inferior deities. At least, on some islands, these were supposed to be incarnate in certain objects, particularly animals, which they regarded with religious veneration. In this way, in some groups, a great variety of animals, the eel, the shark, the dog, all kinds of fishes and birds and creeping things, even shell-fish, would be the representative of some god. His worshippers would not injure or treat with contempt the creature in which he resided, and eating it they would fear as causing sudden death, though they would freely partake of the animal inhabited by the gods of others. They had also gods represented by natural objects, as the rainbow, or the shooting star, and, among the Hawaiians, gods residing in the volcano, who were the objects of fearful terror. Sometimes villages and districts had their gods, households had theirs, and even individuals were put from birth under the protection of a tutelary divinity. Very often these deities were the spirits of distinguished men.

These gods they feared as causing death and other calamities in their wrath, and to appease them they made large offerings, cooked food being the most common. But on special occasions human sacrifices were offered, as among the Hawaiians at the dedication of a temple, when a chief was sick, or on going to war, and such occasions were frequent. In addition, the numerous demands of a cunning and avaricious priesthood rendered the service of their idols extremely burdensome.

One of the institutions which, if not peculiar to Polynesia, had its strongest hold there, both to the East and West, was the tabu. This was a system of prohibitions and restrictions connected with their idolatry laid upon persons, trees and other objects, but especially as to food. On some islands a husband could on no occasion eat with his wife, and women were prohibited from eating the choicest kinds of meat, fish or fruit. The restriction might be arbitrarily imposed by chiefs or sacred men. Thus one of these might tabu a field of taro or other food by placing a stick of sugar-cane in one corner, and then no person would dare to take any of it, even if starving. The penalty for the violation of tabu was death, or, if the guilty party escaped punishment from men, he was deemed certain to suffer the vengeance of their gods.

It was among these races that many supposed for a

time that there were to be found savages living in primeval innocence. It did not require very long or close intercourse with them to dispel the pleasing illusion. They were soon seen to be hateful and hating one another. Lying, theft and robbery were universal, and drunkenness, as far as they had the opportunity. Wars were incessant, during which untold cruelties were inflicted. Men feasted on human flesh, in some cases the heart of the victim being offered in their temples as a religious rite, and by other rites not less bloody were their gods honoured. No man had any security for his property or even for his life. Licentiousness was shameless, not even shunning the light of open day. Men lived with as many wives as they could keep, and for such a time as fancy dictated, and women with several husbands. Thus female virtue was so unknown that the Hawaiians had no word in their language to express it. Hence infanticide, quarrels and murder were common, so that from these causes on many islands the population was diminishing. A virus also was introduced into their blood, which rendered them an easy prey to foreign epidemics. Such was the condition of these "innocent savages," which it has been regarded as a pity to disturb by the introduction among them of Christian civilization.

All the leading groups inhabited by the Sawiori race have been christianized, with the exception of the Marquesas, though perhaps some remnants of heathenism are to be found in them all. Good progress has also been made in missions to the Tarapons. We therefore pass on to consider the other portion of the Pacific Islands, yet to a large extent in unbroken heathenism.

SECTION II. WESTERN POLYNESIA.

This includes the groups of islands from the Fijis on the East to New Caledonia on the West and South, and to New Guinea on the North. It includes New Caledonia, the Loyalty Islands, the New Hebrides, the Solomon Islands, New Britain, New Ireland, and besides many smaller islands, New Guinea, the largest in the world after Australia, being 1,600 miles long and in some places 400 wide.* These islands, in number, size and population, far exceed those of the Eastern division.

They are generally inhabited by a race very distinct from that which we have described as occupying Eastern Polynesia. At some points we find intrusive colonies of the latter, and on some islands an intermixture has taken place. But in general, the inhabitants of these groups may be readily distinguished from the others, being more allied to the negro race, and probably of an African or Hamitic origin. They have been known as the Papuan or Austral negro race, but recently the term Melanesian has been applied to them, and is now commonly adopted.

They are physically inferior to the Sawiori race.

---

* The aborigines of Australia are also considered a branch of this race.

They have curly or frizzly hair, a very dark, rough skin, and somewhat of a negro cast of countenance The inhabitants of the Fijis, however, a group of about 250 islands, 80 of which are inhabited, situated at the extreme Eastern limit of the Papuan race, have an average physical development above that of Englishmen.

There is an impression that the work of the missions in the South Seas is nearly complete, but the fact is, the number of islands christianized will not compare in extent or population with those still in heathenism. Among those inhabited by the Papuan race, the Fijis and a few islands in the Loyalty and New Hebrides groups are the only ones evangelized, on some others the work is barely commenced, while many of the largest and most populous are in unbroken Paganism. In these the system appears in its lowest forms, and its unhappy votaries in the most barbarous and degraded condition, perhaps, of any people on the face of the earth. We shall therefore give a more particular account of their moral and religious condition, as showing how low humanity, rejecting the true God, may sink, and also to what depths the gospel may reach to seize and elevate the fallen.

The superstitions of these people differ in detail, not only on every group, but on almost every island, and even in more limited districts; but we have particular accounts by the Rev. John Geddie, first missionary to the New Hebrides, of the state of the people as he found them, especially on Aneiteum, and by Messrs.

Williams and Calvert of the heathenism of the Fijis; and their accounts will give a correct general view of the religious ideas and condition of the islands yet in heathen darkness.

Any idea they may have of one supreme Being is very indistinct, but they have gods many and lords many. In some cases there will be found one god greater than the others. Thus, on Aneiteum, there was one god whose supremacy was acknowledged over the whole island, who it was supposed made men, and who was regarded with such reverence that the natives trembled to mention his name. But what they chiefly had to do with was a multitude of inferior gods of different ranks. On the Fijis they were of two classes, the one immortal, who might properly be called gods, the other deified mortals.

The power of these gods was limited as to locality, the higher presiding over islands and larger districts, the inferior over tribes and families, or over particular trades, as carpenters and fishermen, and even over individuals, every chief having his god, which he sometimes supposed to follow him wherever he went. The Aneiteumese had gods presiding over useful plants, others over animals, others over the various elements and phenomena of nature, the sea, the wind, the thunder, the stream, etc. Altogether so numerous were their gods that Mr. Geddie never found an Aneiteumese who could enumerate them all, and they were believed to out-number the inhabitants themselves.

The Fijian also peopled with invisible beings every remarkable spot, especially the lonely dell, the gloomy cave, and the recesses of the forest, and he supposed them ready to spring out upon him and do him harm, and hence stepped lightly and made offerings as he passed such places. He was much afraid of apparitions, and supposed the spirits of the dead able to do him injury. Hence persons sometimes hid themselves some days after a death, till they thought the spirit was at rest. Mr. Williams says that the Fijians do not worship the heavenly bodies, but the Aneiteumese give the sun and moon a high place among their gods.

They have no idols, properly so called; that is, they make no images of their gods, but they have a variety of sacred objects to which they render reverence. These are commonly stones, though sometimes of wood, but they regard them as the residence of the spirit. On Aneiteum these stones were rough, with a piece chipped off or a depression in some part of it for the ingress or the egress of the resident. Animals too were held sacred, but properly as the shrine of a divinity, though as in all violations of the second commandment the tendency is that the worship should pass from the god to the object representing it.

On the New Hebrides they were found most devoted in their worship. Every other pursuit was dependent upon their religion. If a man commenced a plantation, or went to fish, or undertook a journey, or made a feast, he honoured the occasion by an offering to the proper god. These offerings consisted of pigs, fish, and vegetables of various kinds, accompanied with prayers, and on some islands on special occasions human sacrifices were presented. But on Fiji cannibalism was a part of their religious worship. Of the offerings of food it was believed that the soul was devoured by the gods, who were regarded as great eaters, while the substance was consumed by the worshippers; and it was regarded as one indication of the superiority of certain gods that they delighted in human flesh. "At one time," says Mr. Williams, "Ndengei would constantly have human bodies for his sacrifices; with each basket of roots a man or woman's body was to be brought, and chiefs sometimes killed their inferior wives to supply the horrible demand."

But, practically, their gods are the sacred men. There is among them that part of Shamanism, which regards certain men as having the power of drawing down the power of the gods. These men are supposed to be the servants or agents of invisible powers, and to be able to command the powers of nature, either for destruction or mercy. Thus there are rain-makers, thunder-makers, fly and mosquito makers, but, above all, disease-makers. The belief is invincible in the power of these men, and it is scarcely conceivable the fear which the natives have of incurring their displeasure, and how they submit to every imposition lest they should suffer from their maledictions.

Everywhere there is constant terror of witchcraft. No superstition has such an influence over their minds, and it is the last thing they get rid of when they become converted to Christianity. Persons practising it seek by such processes as burning the hair, or refuse food of the party aimed at, compounding certain leaves having a magic virtue, placing them in a bamboo case and burying them in his garden, or hiding them in the thatch of his house, etc., to bewitch or injure him. All disease is believed to be caused in such ways, and when a person feels affected the course adopted by himself and his friends is to seek to discover and execute vengeance upon the party supposed to cause the evil. And such is the prevalent dread of these charms that a native, learning that he has been put under them, has laid down on his mat and died through fear.

On all the islands there is a belief in a future state. The people on each have a different idea of the road to it, and the condition of the spirits there. But it is a characteristic of all their systems that good and evil is awarded not according to man's moral conduct here. Thus, on the Fijis, it is supposed that there is a god who devours every bachelor who arrives in Hades, and that the man who has not killed an enemy is doomed to what the natives regard as the most ignominious punishment, beating a heap of filth with his club.

Altogether their worship is the manifestation of abject fear. They have no idea of their gods as beings of love. The only credit the Fijians give their gods for kindness is in planting wild yams and in sending shipwrecked vessels and canoes on their coasts. Otherwise they regard all their gods as malicious, easily provoked, and powerful to harm, so that they serve them only from fear of their wrath, and thus their worship affords them no happiness. "To realize somewhat of their condition," writes a missionary, "let us suppose that all our knowledge of God, angels, and spirits—every idea that we have obtained respecting them from the Bible were to be blotted out from our mind—that all this light were to be wanting, and that all we knew of the spiritual world was learned from fabulous legends about ghosts, apparitions, and the appearances and doings of Satan; and suppose that we had an hereditary belief that every noted man was a wizard, and every noted woman a witch, possessed of such powers that by a few incantations they could bring famine, disease or death as often as they would, if it were possible for us to realize such a state of feeling, we should have some faint idea of the grievous fear engendered by heathenism."

MORAL CONDITION.

In regard to this we shall quote Dr. Geddie's account of the state of the inhabitants of the New Hebrides, which is still applicable to those islands not yet visited by the gospel.

"All society in these dark regions is indeed a Dead Sea of pollution. The Apostle Paul, in his epistle to the Romans (chap. i. 29-31), gives a faithful and awful delineation of heathen character. This is but imperfectly understood in Christian lands. Much that might be affirmed of those who inhabit these dark regions must be witnessed to be believed. There are few missionaries who could not place emphasis on every sentence of the apostle's description of heathenism, and clothe every word in capitals. Can we indeed expect anything from the poor heathen when their deities are supposed to be such as themselves, or rather are conceived of as having attained to a more gigantic stature in every form of vice than man can possibly reach? Crimes of all degrees and of every kind are of constant occurrence among these islanders. Selfishness, treachery and inhumanity are among the traits of character so prominent that a short acquaintance with the people brings them to light. Falsehood is more common than the truth, and a native will often lie when the truth would seem better to ensure his purpose. Theft is not at all disreputable, and parents will teach their children to steal, and then applaud them for their expertness if successful. Licentiousness is a besetting sin, and society has become a perfect chaos in consequence of its prevalence. Filial respect is not expected by parents from their children, nor is it given. Cruelty and bloodshed excite no more horror than events of the most common occurrence. Revenge is considered a sacred duty, means are taken to preserve the memory of an injury even to after generations, and generally they have no word for forgiveness in their language. The language of impiety and impurity is so common that a native can scarcely speak without blending his ordinary conversation with it.

"There are few places on the earth where the female sex is more degraded than among these islands. As physical strength and personal valour are the qualities most admired by a barbarous people, the weaker sex are despised and trampled on." We must omit the particulars, but note Mr. Geddie's concluding sentence. "The spectacle of a father and mother with their children, as one social happy band, is what I have never yet beheld in this dark region."

But one feature of life on some islands must be mentioned—the strangling of widows. On Aneiteum, when a woman was married, a strong cord was fastened around her neck. If her husband died, this was immediately used to strangle her, that her spirit might accompany his to the land of darkness, and all her children unable to provide for themselves shared the same fate. If there was a son of competent age, he was expected to perform the murderous ceremony of strangling his mother. If not, the duty devolved on her brother, or, failing him, on the nearest relation, it might be a daughter. Mr. Geddie had at one time on his premises a woman who had strangled her own mother. The honour of all connected, and especially of those on whom devolved the work of execution, rendered the deed necessary, and even the woman was often bent on her own destruction. It may be observed, as showing how the worst practices of heathenism result from the perversion of the best principles, that in this custom the parties were really acting under the influence of natural affection.

Widows, however, were not the only persons strangled on the occasion of a death. Sometimes a mother was strangled to accompany her son. An instance came under Dr. Geddie's notice, where a young man and woman were strangled on the death of a chief's wife, and of two women being strangled when the child of a person of rank died.

On the Fijis the practice was equally prevalent, and from the greater power of the chiefs, and the consequent larger number of their wives, it was even more destructive, as these were all involved in the same fate. In addition, in the case of a chief, his confidential companion would be considered as acting a very undutiful part if he did not yield himself as a sacrifice. Mr. Williams mentions the case of a chief of high rank and held in esteem, who died in 1840, when, besides his own wife, five men and their wives were slain as " grass for his grave," as they express it, and of another who was lost at sea, when seventeen of his wives were strangled.

It has been said, indeed, that the women who were destroyed were sacrificed at their own desire. But in reality they knew that life would henceforth be to them prolonged insult, neglect and want. They knew, too, that their parents and friends had determined on their death. The courage they manifested was forced, or the result of despair, which sees in death a refuge from the suffering and wrong awaiting the woman who survives her husband.

On many islands the aged are regularly put to death. Grey hairs and bald heads, instead of being regarded as an honour, excite only contempt. An idea is entertained that as they die, so will they be in the other world, and this is made the excuse for a regular system of cutting short their days. Sick persons, if they have no friends, are simply left to perish, but those that have friends, if in two or three days they do not recover, are put out of the way, commonly by being buried alive, and when this is determined upon appeals are useless. It is sad to add that there is truth in the reason assigned for this practice; that such is the malignity of the sick, that when left alone they will lie on the mats of their friends, mix saliva with their food, or take any other measures that they think will be the means of communicating the disease to the healthy members of the household.

The disregard of human life, and the cruelty which characterizes the Papuan race generally, is almost incredible. We give a few specimens from the Fijis. When a chief's house was to be built, a series of holes were dug for the main posts. Then, as soon as these were placed in position, a man was compelled to descend into each and grasp the posts in his arms, when the earth was filled in, and he was buried alive. It was also the practice that a chief should kill a man on laying down the keel of a new canoe, and aim also at one for each new plank. These were always eaten as "food for the carpenters," and at the launching living men were placed as rollers, over whom it was hauled, their bodies being afterward disposed of in the same way. When a chief visited another district, the taking down of the mast was expected to be honoured by the killing of a man or men. They are an extremely polite people, but the slightest breach of etiquette might bring the deadly blow. We have heard of murder as a fine art, but it was the glory of every Fijian. To be known as having killed some person, high or low, young or old, man, woman or child, in war or by treachery, was his earliest ambition. An honorary name was given when he first accomplished the feat, and in due recognition of the honour he must soon "wash his club," as it is expressed, or commit another murder. A missionary asked a man how he had received his new title, and was told in reply, "I with several other men found some women and children in a cave, drew them out, clubbed them, and then was *consecrated*." But every murder is likely to lead to others. If the man killed was married his wife would be strangled, if not, perhaps his mother. On one occasion there had been a fearful massacre of the people of one village, when upwards of 100 fishermen had been murdered, and their bodies carried away for food. As a sequel 80 widows were strangled, and their bodies lay strown around the mission station.

From such a state of things it may be supposed that they live in a state of constant fear. There is in fact no security for life or property. Such is the state of hostility in which they live that a native of an island ten miles long may never have seen the length of it, and it may be death for him to pass the boundary of his own district, perhaps from two to four miles long. Wars are almost constant, not because the people are warlike, but from a desire to obtain their neighbour's property, from pride or revenge, and not unfrequently from a simple desire to obtain human bodies as food. They are carried on by treacherous plots rather than by open fighting, and attended by the most heartless cruelty, women and children being slaughtered in the most barbarous manner.

Their cannibalism has been incidentally referred to. Of the 300 or more islands inhabited by the Papuan race, not one has yet been found on which it did not exist. It is not an occasional thing, nor an act committed for revenge in war time; it is interwoven with their whole social system. Instead of exciting disgust it is regarded with satisfaction. Not only are all victims killed or taken in war the lawful food of the victors, strangers thrown upon their shores, natives of other islands who have drifted thither, even natives of their own islands who have landed in another district, and shipwrecked seamen are alike cooked and eaten. It was also common for chiefs to kill men for the sake of eating them. In one district Dr. Geddie found very few children, and learned that the reason was that the chief had killed and eaten them. But men also were killed as his appetite impelled, so that the people were afraid to sleep in their houses at night. Dr. Geddie knew a man who killed and ate his own child. The Rev. R. Lyth gives an account of a great Fijian chief who stood up a stone for each body that he had eaten, and by actual count they were found to be 872.

Yet these Fijians and some of the New Hebrides islanders have, through the power of the gospel of Jesus Christ, become Christian communities. "What hath God wrought!"

CHAPTER IX.

THE HEATHEN IN AMERICA.

"They that dwell in the wilderness shall bow before Him."—Psalm lxxii. 9.

IT is impossible to obtain anything like accurate information in regard to the number of heathen in America. Many of the aboriginal races have become partially, and a few wholly Christian; but a large proportion are still in heathenism, perhaps a little modified in some instances for the better, but in many for the worse, by contact with the whites. Then we have heathen being introduced as immigrants—Coolies from the East into the West India Islands and the adjoining regions of South America, and Chinese into California and British Columbia. Bainbridge estimates the total number of heathen in North and South America as follows:

Hindoos	86,000
Buddhists, etc., (Chinese or Japanese)	152,000
Pagans	9,244,000
Religions not specified	166,000
	9,648,000

By pagans he means those who have no religious books. The number given as Hindoos is too small.

THE HEATHEN IN AMERICA. 173

Perhaps we will not be making too high an estimate in reckoning them altogether as ten millions, independent of negroes, who have professed Christianity, but who retain much of their old heathenism. The large majority of these are in South America. Little, however, is known of their condition.

Of the Hindoos and Chinese we have already given an account, and in regard to the aboriginal tribes of North America it may be sufficient to refer to those in the Dominion of Canada.

To the North we have the Eskimos, who also occupy Greenland. They are found from the Eastern side of that country to the Western shores of Alaska, a distance of 3,200 miles. As to their numbers, we have somewhat correct statistics as to Greenland, where they are about 10,000, but how many are to be found in the rest of the region mentioned is altogether uncertain, probably not more than 40,000.

The following is a short account of their religious ideas, as given by Dr. Robert Brown, in an article in the "Encyclopedia Britannica:" "The whole world is governed by *inuas*, supernatural powers, or 'owners,' each of whom holds its sway within natural limits. Any object or individual may have its, his or her *inua*, though, generally speaking, the idea of an *inua* is limited to certain localities or passions, such as a mountain or lake, or strength or eating. The soul, for instance, is the *inua* of the body. The earth and the sea rest on pillars, and cover an under-world accessible by various mountain clefts, or by various entrances from the sea. The sky is the floor of an upper-world, to which some go after death, while others, good or bad, have their future home in the under-world. Here are the dwellings of the *arsissut*, the people who live in abundance. The upper one, on the contrary, is cold and hungry. Here live the *arssartut* or ball-players, so called from their playing at ball with a walrus head, which gives rise to the aurora borealis The mediums between the *inua* and mankind are the *angakoks* (Esk. plur. angakut) or wizards, who possess the peculiar gift of *angakoonek*, or the state of 'being angakok,' which they have acquired by the aid of guardian spirits called *tomat* (plural of tomak), who again are ruled by *tomarsuk*, the supreme deity, or devil of all. They also invoke a supernatural influence, which is called *kusiunek* or *iliseenek*, which may be translated witchcraft. This is believed to be the mystic agency which causes sudden sickness or death."

In Greenland and Labrador the Moravians and Danish missionaries have laboured successfully among them, but nearly all those in other places are in their original heathenism, though we have observed that recently an Episcopal mission has been established among them far into the interior and within the Arctic circle.

As to the other aboriginal tribes in the Dominion, those in the Maritime Provinces are all Roman Catholics, and of those in Ontario and Quebec a large portion have embraced either the Protestant or Romish faith, though some still remain heathen. In the

North-West, through the efforts of Christian missionaries, especially of the Church of England and Wesleyan bodies, a number have become Christians. In the whole Dominion we suppose that the number of pagan Indians will amount to 100,000. In a great part of the North-West, through contact with the whites, they have laid aside some of the worst of their heathen practices, but in the more distant portions of it, and through the northern parts of British Columbia, as well as through Alaska, large tribes are still found practising some of the worst abominations of heathenism. The following particulars are derived from a work on Alaska by Rev. Dr. Sheldon Jackson, of the American Presbyterian Home Mission Board, published in 1880:

Their system of religion is a feeble polytheism, or a sort of Shamanism. They generally have an idea of one god superior to the rest, but he occupies only a small place in their worship. Among the people of one tribe he is represented as having let the sun, moon and stars out of boxes, in which they were kept by a rich chief, and having provided fire and water, and arranged everything for the comfort of the Indians, then disappeared, where neither man nor spirit can penetrate. But they believe in an immense number of minor spirits, which fill the earth, the air and the waters, some of them the spirits of departed men, those of the brave who have been slain in battle being of high rank. Some of these spirits are good, but the majority are supposed to be evil, and on the watch to do them harm. As they think that the good spirits will not do them any harm, they do not trouble themselves about them, but they seek by offerings to the evil to prevent them doing mischief to the offerer. Thus in reality, as the apostle says, " they sacrifice to demons and not to God."

These spirits are supposed to be under the control of the sorcerer or medicine-man of the tribe, and the more he has at his disposal, the greater his power. Through them he is supposed to cause diseases, or to have the fortunes of men at his disposal, though to accomplish his ends he must go through some disgusting or horrible rites. Thus all the Indians are kept in abject dread of these men. Their command is law, and the contributions, extorted through fear, enable them to live in abundance, while their victims may be in want.

Bancroft in his " Native Races on the Pacific Coast," thus speaks of Shamanism :

" Thick black clouds, portenteous of evil, hang threateningly over the savage during his entire life. Genii murmur in the flowing river; in the rustling branches of trees are heard the breathing of the gods; goblins dance in the vapoury twilight, and demons howl in the darkness. All these beings are hostile to man, and must be propitiated by gifts and prayers and sacrifices; and the religious worship of some of the tribes includes practices which are frightful in their atrocity. Here, for example, is a rite of sorcery as practised among the Haidahs, one of the Northern nations:

"When the salmon season is over, and the provisions of winter have been stored away, feasting and conjuring begin. The chief, who seems to be principal sorcerer, and indeed to possess little authority save for his connection with the superhuman powers, goes off to the loneliest and wildest retreat he knows of, or can discover in the mountains or forests, and half starves himself there for some weeks, till he is worked up to a frenzy of religious insanity, and the *nawloks*—fearful beings of some kind, not human—consent to communicate with him by voices or otherwise. During all this observance the chief is called *taamish*, and woe to the unlucky Haidah who happens by chance so much as to look on him during its continuance! Even if the *taamish* do not instantly slay the intruder, his neighbours are certain to do so when the thing comes to their knowledge, and if the victim attempts to conceal the affair, or do not himself confess it, the most cruel tortures are added to his fate. At last the inspired demoniac returns to his village naked, save a bear skin or a ragged blanket, with a chaplet on his head, and a red band of alder bark about his neck. He springs on the first person he meets, bites out and swallows one or more mouthfuls of the man's living flesh, wherever he can fix his teeth, then rushes to another and another, repeating his revolting meal till he falls into a torpor from his sudden and half-masticated surfeit of flesh. For some days after this he lies in a kind of coma, like an over-gorged beast of prey, the same observer adding that his breath during that time is like an exhalation from the grave. The victims of his ferocity dare not resist the bite of the *taamish*; on the contrary, they are sometimes willing to offer themselves to the ordeal, and are always proud of its scars."

The influence of British or American authority has checked some of their most cruel practices, but the first visitors soon learned enough to feel that those lands were "the habitations of horrid cruelty." Tribal wars were continual, bloodshed and murder of daily occurrence. When the corner posts of the larger dwellings were placed in position, a slave was murdered and placed under each. When the houses were completed and occupied, slaves, according to the wealth of the owner, were butchered. In the case of a powerful chief, the victims might be reckoned by the score, the object being to show his grandeur—that he could afford to kill and yet have plenty left. "Founded and dedicated with human sacrifices," says Dr. Jackson, "who can conceive of the aggregate of woe and suffering in those habitations of cruelty, year after year, at the wild drunken orgies of the Indians, their horrid cannibal feasts, their inhuman torture of witches, their fiendish carousals around the burning dead, the long, despairing wails of lost souls as they passed out into eternal darkness."

Nor are these scenes things of the past. Writing in 1880, Mr. Jackson says: "There are villages on this coast (British Columbia) where these same scenes of blood and cruelty are still enacted." Mr. William Duncan, who went out as a teacher in 1857, and whose successful labours at Methlakatla are well known, thus depicts some of the scenes which he witnessed shortly after his arrival:

"The other day we were called to witness a terrible scene. An old chief, in cold blood, ordered a slave to be dragged to the beach, murdered and thrown into the water. His orders were quickly obeyed. The victim was a poor woman. Two or three reasons were assigned for this foul act. One is, that it is to take away the disgrace attached to his daughter, who had been suffering for some time with a ball wound in the arm. Another report is, that he does not expect his daughter to recover, so he has killed this slave in order that she may prepare for the coming of his daughter into the unseen world. I did not see the murder, but immediately after saw crowds of people running out of the houses, near to where the corpse was thrown, and forming themselves in groups at a good distance away, from fear of what was to follow. Presently two bands of furious wretches appeared, each headed by a man in a state of nudity. They gave vent to the most unearthly sounds, and the naked men made themselves look as unearthly as possible.... For some time they pretended to be looking for the body, and the instant they came where it lay, they commenced screaming and rushing around it like so many angry wolves. Finally, they seized it, dragged it out of the water, and laid it on the beach, where they commenced tearing it to pieces with their teeth. The two bands of men immediately surrounded them, and so hid their horrid work. In a few minutes the crowd broke again, when each of the naked cannibals appeared with half the body in his hands. Separating a few yards, they commenced, amid horrid yells, their still more horrid feast of eating the raw dead body. The two bands of men belonged to that class called 'medicine-men.'"

"I may mention that each party has some characteristic peculiar to itself; but in a more general sense their divisions are but three, viz., those who eat human bodies, the dog-eaters, and those who have no custom of the kind." . . . "Of all these parties, none are so much dreaded as the cannibals. One morning I was called to witness a stir in the camp, which had been caused by this set. When I reached the gallery, I saw hundreds of Tsimpseans sitting in their canoes, which they had just pushed away from the beach. I was told that the cannibal party were in search of a body to devour, and if they failed to find a dead one, it was probable they would seize the first living one that came in their way; so that all the people living near the cannibals' house had taken to their canoes, to escape being torn to pieces. It is the custom among these Indians to burn their dead, but I suppose for these occasions they take care to deposit a corpse somewhere, in order to satisfy these inhuman wretches."

In some tribes the old and feeble are put to death. This is done by placing a rope around their necks, and dragging them over the stones. If this fail to destroy life, they are stoned or speared, and left to be eaten by the dogs.

But, as usual in heathenism, the chief burden of sorrow rests upon the female sex. Such is the wretchedness of their lives, that many mothers, to save their daughters from similar wretchedness, put them to death in infancy. The Rev. W. W. Kirby, of the Church Missionary Society, who passed through the Canadian North-West to the Upper Yukon, says: " In common with all savage people, the Indians regard their women as slaves, and compel them to do the hardest work, while they look lazily on, enjoying the luxury of a pipe, and often requite their service with harsh words and cruel blows. They are inferior in looks and fewer in number than the men. The former probably arises from the harsh treatment they receive, and the latter is caused in a great measure by the too prevalent custom of infanticide. Many a poor mother assured me that she had killed her child to save it from suffering the misery she had herself endured. . . . Then came the sad and harrowing tales of murder and infanticide. No fewer than thirteen women confessed to having slain their infant girls, some in the most cruel and heartless manner."

If spared in infancy, they are soon made to feel the wretchedness of their condition. Even in girlhood their brothers will make them carry their burdens, and devolve their work upon them. When little more than babes, they are sometimes given away or betrothed to their future husbands. Heathenism turns even a mother's heart to stone, and when her daughter reaches the age of twelve or fourteen years, she will, sometimes for a few blankets, sell her for base purposes, for a week, or a month, or even for life. *

After marriage, they are practically slaves to their husbands. Among some tribes, all the labour except hunting and fighting is laid upon them. Polygamy is common among the rich, who will multiply their wives in the same spirit as a farmer does his oxen. The more he has the more wood he can have cut, and the more goods hauled or carried. One chief is reported to have had forty. Among some tribes their persons are at the disposal of visitors or travellers. In the neighbourhood of the mines they are sent among the miners, while the husband lives at home in idleness upon the wages of their immorality. Sometimes they are traded off for anything he may desire. Even their lives are at his disposal. "During our visit to Fort Wrangell in 1879," says Mr. Jackson, "an Indian killed his wife and brought her body into the village for a funeral. No one could interfere. According to their customs, he had bought her as he would buy a dog, and if he chose he could kill as he would kill a dog."

The majority of the slaves are women. The men

---

* This practice caused no little trouble in the first mission schools in Alaska, the more promising girls being sold by their own mothers and with difficulty saved.

captured are usually killed or reserved for torture, while the women are kept as beasts of burden at the will of cruel masters, who may even torture or kill them. Sometimes a female slave is offered in sacrifice, and till recently it has been the practice, and probably in some places is yet, that on the death of the master, a number of them, according to his wealth, should be slain to attend him in the other world, so that he may be saved from all labour there.

In these circumstances it is not surprising that many females seek a refuge from their sorrows in suicide.

Mr. Jackson concludes by giving the following testimony to the accuracy of his statements, from Mr. E. Morgan, for many years a Christian captain of a whaling vessel :—

"I have read all that my brother Sheldon Jackson has published concerning Alaska, and I know of but one mistake he makes. He does not say enough. He has not told you one-half of the degradation of these Northern Indians."

CONCLUSION.

WE have thus gone over the earth, measuring the length and breadth of heathenism, and casting our plummet here and there into its depths. We have welcomed any light we could find that would relieve the darkness, and we have not sought in any way to exaggerate the evils which it presents. On the contrary, the testimony of missionaries in every quarter of the world is, that the moral corruption of the heathen must be witnessed to be believed. But even on the review we have taken, sad and sickening has been the spectacle. We behold the majority of our race sunk in "abominable idolatries," giving the honour that belongs to the true God to the creatures of His hand, or to objects fashioned by themselves, yea, even to sticks and to stones. We see them rendering services irrational in their absurdity, or insulting to the Holy One of Israel, by their cruelty and impurity, and of which the effects can only be debasing to the offerer. Moreover, as the result, we see them sunk in the vilest immorality, while the stoniest heart might melt at the contemplation of their wretchedness, the intellect unsatisfied by all its enquiries, the heart finding no rest for its anxious disquietudes, "their sorrows multiplied" through the raging of human passions and the prevalence of practices tending to dissolve the very framework of society; and life, so far from being brightened by the prospect of deliverance in the future, darkened by the sad experience that, being "without God," they are "without hope in the world."

Can we add anything to the blackness of the picture? Alas, we might write a chapter, every line of it in colours as dark as any we have written, to describe the evil influence upon the heathen of men from civilized and Christian countries. Bad as is the moral condition of the heathen left to themselves, it has been rendered worse in every part of the world accessible to trade, by the conduct of men who have gone from gospel lands. In cruelty and licentiousness they have rivalled the most besotted idolaters, and made the name of white men and Christians a term of obloquy, while their vices have inoculated whole tribes with disease, which is in some instances cutting them off from the earth.

It is important that the exact condition of the heathen should be fully realized by all engaged in any way in the work of Foreign Missions. When the Church in modern times awoke to a sense of her duty to them, the strongest appeals were made to her sympathies on their behalf, and she engaged in the work of sending them the gospel with great earnestness, but often with a very inadequate conception of the depths of depravity in which they are sunk, and the firmness of the hold which evil habits had upon their minds. Agents, too, went forth in ignorance of the difficulties to be encountered, and, in a measure, unprepared to meet them. The result frequently was disappointment. Instead of the gospel, which she was offering them with a full heart, being joyfully accepted, she found the wickedness of the human heart manifested at first in the scornful rejection of its claims. Agents were disappointed. Some who were only sustained by sentimental sympathy abandoned the work. Others had to moderate their expectations, and, with new views of human depravity, to summon up stronger faith, and bend to their work with more resolute patience than they had previously counted necessary. And when the gospel did succeed, and churches were gathered from among the heathen, Christians at home and missionaries abroad were both disappointed that the converts did not at once rise to the spiritual stature of Christians in Britain and America, inheritors of eighteen centuries of Christianity, and were even surprised to find among them outbreaks of such depravity as disfigured the Church of Corinth, or such instability as was found among the Galatians. Even yet they need to be well informed on the subject, that they may be prepared to put forth the sustained efforts which the work requires, that instead of becoming discouraged they may maintain the patience and perseverance through which alone they may expect to reap, and especially that they may be roused to take hold of that Almighty strength by which alone their efforts will be successful.

It only remains on this part of our subject to show the extent of heathenism, by noting the number of its votaries, as compared with those of other systems of religion. Correct statistics cannot be obtained, and various estimates have been made. That of Bainbridge is probably as near the truth as any. It is as follows:—

	EUROPE.	ASIA.	AFRICA.	AMERICA.	OCEANICA.	TOTAL.
Jews	5,437,000	1,005,000	938,000	137,000	10,000	7,527,000
Mohammedans	5,974,000	112,739,000	50,416,000	....	....	169,129,000
Hindoos, including aboriginal races	....	176,312,000	275,000	86,000	....	176,673,000
Buddhists, Taouists, Confucianists, Shintos, and Jains	....	502,363,000	2,000	152,000	30,000	502,547,000
Miscellaneous and not specified	211,000	8,304,000	....	166,000	295,000	8,976,000
Pagans*	258,000	12,029,000	144,729,000	9,244,000	2,393,000	168,653,000
Total non-Christian	11,880,000	812,752,000	196,360,000	9,785,000	2,728,000	1,033,505,000
Roman Catholics	150,223,000	1,429,000	669,000	37,540,000	454,000	190,315,000
Protestants	75,124,000	430,000	740,000	37,380,000	1,544,000	115,218,000
Greek Church	71,588,000	6,370,000	....	....	....	77,958,000
Armenians, Copts, and Abyssinians	255,000	2,684,000	1,650,000	....	....	4,589,000
Other Christians not specified	110,000	1,013,000	501,000	815,000	22,600	2,461,600
Total Christians	297,300,000	11,926,000	3,560,000	75,737,000	2,020,600	390,541,600
Grand total	309,180,000	824,678,000	199,920,000	85,520,000	4,748,600	1,424,046,600

* By this term he distinguishes those destitute of any literary culture.

PART II.

THE HEATHEN'S NEED OF THE GOSPEL.

"Where there is no vision, the people perish."—Prov. xxix. 18.

THE HEATHEN'S NEED OF THE GOSPEL.

"As many as have sinned without law, shall also perish without law."—Rom. ii. 12.

FROM the condition of the heathen, as we have found them everywhere and under all circumstances, their need of the gospel of salvation is the first and necessary conclusion. If they are diseased and dying, they surely need the physician and the remedy. This leads us to the very solemn enquiry as to their position before God, as the great Lawgiver, and their eternal future. This is a subject from the examination of which we are naturally inclined to shrink, and at any time it becomes us to approach the consideration of it with a holy awe upon our spirits. But the question is one of fact, not of feeling; and it is unworthy of us as Christian enquirers to evade it, or to refuse to examine it because of its painfulness. If the Scriptures give us information on the subject, it is not a true charity to hide from ourselves or others the conclusions to which it leads. Let us, then "seek out of the Book of the Lord, and read" what, God Himself hath testified on this momentous question.

SECTION I.—IDOLATRY A HEINOUS SIN BEFORE GOD.

And here, first, we think that every candid reader of the Bible must have been struck with the constancy and the vehemence with which it represents *idolatry, as* SIN *the most offensive in the sight of God ;* alike the fruit of a depraved heart and the seed of all evil:

"Thou shalt have no other gods before me."

"Thou shalt not make unto thee any graven image, or any likeness of any thing that is in heaven above, or that is in the earth beneath, or that is in the water under the earth: thou shalt not bow down thyself to them, nor serve them: for I the Lord thy God am a jealous God, visiting the iniquity of the fathers upon the children unto the third and fourth generation of them that hate me; and shewing mercy unto thousands of them that love me, and keep my commandments."

These were the first utterances of the Most High, when He came down to make known His laws to His creatures. They stood at the head of the law of the Ten Commandments, which He wrote with His own finger on two tables of stone, to be laid up in the ark of the testimony through all the generations of Israel. Thus, when "the law was given by Moses," "glory to God in the highest" was the first note in the song, as when grace and truth came by Jesus Christ. By the position of these precepts, we are taught that His own honour stands first in the mind of the Supreme, as it must be the first principle of action with all His loving subjects. Our duty to Him is thus made the first of obligations resting upon us and the foundation of all others.

It will be observed that each of these commandments forbids a *class* of sins, and teaches the corresponding positive duties by condemning *the chief sin of the kind*. So in these first two precepts which respect our duty to God, He condemns the two great characteristic forms of idolatry, the worshipping other beings than the true God, and the worshipping Him through material objects or visible representations—a practice which has, under all circumstances, led to giving these representations the honour at first intended for the object represented, thus marking these as the most open and flagrant violations of our duty to Him.

The importance which the Almighty attaches to this part of human obligation appears in the solemn manner in which He upholds and enforces it. He first asserts His sole and supreme authority. "For I am the Lord thy God." If the importance of any principle may be known by the frequency with which it is repeated in Scripture, none can be more important than this. But He specially declares that from His very nature He must vindicate His lawful authority as against idolatry. "I the Lord thy God am a jealous God." "Jealousy is cruel as the grave; the coals thereof are coals of fire, which hath a most vehement flame." Excluding what of human infirmity may mark this passion among men, language could not more strongly express the displeasure with which the Most High regards the dishonour done to Him by heathen worship. This jealousy finds its expression in the certain punishment of the transgressor: "Visiting the iniquity of the fathers upon the children.' This, of course, is on the supposition that the children follow the evil conduct of their parents, which, from the propagating power of sin, they are, in the ordinary course of events, likely to do. How this is realized is seen in the deepening debasement of one generation after another in heathenism, exposing them more and more to the displeasure of Him who "will not give His glory to another, nor His praise to graven images."

In this view we are brought into collision with a form of modern philosophy. Men "professing themselves to be wise" claim to have risen above such an idea. They find in all the forms of worship among men only the working of "the natural instinct of religion." Accordingly they regard all religious adoration—the Fetich worshipper bowing to a stick, the Hindoo mother throwing her child into the Ganges, the Fijian holding a cannibal feast on an offering to his god, the Grecian maiden prostituting herself to a stranger in the temple of Aphrodite, or the lover of the Saviour offering the spiritual worship of the New Testament—as services perhaps not quite equally elevated, but of the same character, and almost equally acceptable or equally indifferent, to the unknown God.

We at once admit that in all such observances there is the exercise of a principle natural to man which impels him to religious worship, but to say that there is no essential distinction in worship, whether the object be God or man, a stone or the devil, and whether the services be the obscenity and bloodshed of heathen worship or the pure offerings that become the Holy One of Israel, is to confound all moral distinctions, and is to shut our eyes to the plainest and most earnest teaching of the word of God. Nothing so engages the attention of the Most High in all the revelations of His grace and all the dispensations of his Providence recorded there, as the suppression of idolatry and the establishment of His claim to universal sovereignty.

To establish the truth of the unity of God, and His sole supremacy, especially in opposition to idols, was a first and a main object of the whole Mosaic institute, and of all God's dealings with the children of Israel through the whole period of the Jewish dispensation. With this view, they were separated from the other nations of the earth, that they might be preserved from the contamination of idolatry, and, at the same time, from the central position they occupied, be a standing protest against the Polytheism around. Their settlement in Canaan was by a process which served to mark the abhorrence with which the Most High regarded idol worship, and to train their minds in a similar feeling. The old inhabitants were sunk so low in the vices of heathenism that the righteous, moral Governor of the universe doomed them to utter destruction; and, to impress upon His people more deeply a sense of the evils of the system, appointed them to be the executioners of His vengeance.

Then they were placed under a system of laws, both as to their worship and whole social life, designed to keep them separate from the heathen, and to train them in abhorrence of all idolatry. Not only was the general law against idolatry, laid down in the first and second commandments, repeated on various occasions (Lev. xxvi. 1, Deut. iv. 15-19), and enforced by solemn denunciations of judgment should they disobey it (Deut. iv. 25-27, Lev. xxvi. 1, 21-39), but a variety of particular precepts were given with the same purpose. Any one who sacrificed to an idol was to be put to death. (Exodus xxii. 20.) His nearest relatives were required to denounce him, and their hands were to be first upon him in the execution of the sentence. (Deut. xiii. 6-10.) Sacrificing children to Moloch, instead of being treated with respect, as an expression of the "natural religious instinct," subjected the guilty to the same doom, and that in a way by which the people would express their abhorrence of the deed. (Lev. xx. 2.) They were to destroy all the monuments of idolatry. (Deut. xii. 2, 3.) They were not to desire the silver or gold upon them, for the whole was an abomination unto the Lord. (Deut. vii. 25.) Every practice so far partaking of the nature of idolatry as to involve the idea of some occult power other than that of the Creator ruling the destinies of men, such as enchantment, witchcraft, etc., was to be banished from among them, and even those addicted to such arts were to be put to death. (Deut. xviii. 9-12, Lev. xx. 27.)

To guard them against any temptation to this sin, they were commanded to make no covenant with idolaters and not to intermarry with them. (Exodus xxxiv. 15, 16.) A variety of trivial, and, what we might regard as in themselves absurd, precepts were commanded them which derived their significance and importance from their being directed against idolatrous practices (Exodus xxiii. 19, Lev. xix. 19, 27, 28, Deut. xiv. 1, Deut. xxiii. 5); and they were placed under a minute code of regulations as to food and ceremonial uncleanness which was of itself sufficient to raise a barrier against any close intercourse with idolaters.

The providential dispensations of God with them as a nation through long ages, and with other nations in relation to them, all bore upon the same object. From the day when the plague came upon them for the worship of the golden calf, through all their history every lapse into idolatry brought upon them the judgments of the Almighty, until finally for the same crime they were as a people carried away captive into a foreign land and their civil and ecclesiastical constitution overturned. "Ye have seen all the evil that I have brought upon Jerusalem, and upon all the cities of Judah; and, behold, this day they are a desolation, and no man dwelleth therein, because of their wickedness which they have committed to provoke me to anger, in that *they went to burn incense, and to serve other gods.* Howbeit I sent unto you all my servants the prophets, rising early and sending them, saying, Oh, do not *this abominable thing which I hate.*" (Jer. xliv. 2-4.)

The writings of psalmists and prophets were inspired with the same idea. In them God is everywhere seen proclaiming against the gods many of the heathen, "I am the Lord, and there is none else." The worship of such objects is the perversion of reason, and they pour upon it contempt. "The customs of the people are vain: for one cutteth a tree out of the forest, they deck it with silver and gold; they fasten it with nails and with hammers, that it move not. They must needs be borne, because they cannot go." (See also 1 Kings xviii. 27, 28, Psa. cxv. 5-8, Isa. xliv. 9-20, xlvi. 1, 2.) But if idols are so often represented as "vanity, and molten images as wind and confusion," not less frequently are they represented as "abomination" and the service of them as pre-eminently "*the* evil" in the eyes of the Lord. (1 Kings xxi. 25.) It is an assault upon His supremacy, it is a foul dishonour to His divine perfections and character, giving to the work of men's hand the place of the Creator of all, or substituting the embodiment of all the vilest passions of our own corrupted nature for Him who is benignity, purity and truth. This it is that causes Him to call upon the heavens to "be astonished, to be horribly afraid, and to be very desolate." This it is that stirs the heart of the child of God, as when the prophet exclaimed: "Their land is full of idols, they worship the work of their hands.... therefore forgive them not." (Isa. ii. 8, 9.) While for the practice of its rites the All-merciful pronounced upon His beloved people the tremendous sentence: "Therefore will I also deal in fury; mine eye shall not spare, neither will I have pity, and though they cry in mine ears with a loud voice, yet will I not hear them." (Ezek. viii. 18.)

Not less solemn are the representations given of it in the New Testament. There it is held up as a "manifest work of the flesh" (Gal. v. 20), its services as "abominable" (1 Peter iv. 3), and those practising them as in darkness, "under the power of Satan" (Acts xxvi. 18), "walking according to the prince of the power of the air, the spirit that now worketh in the children of disobedience." (Eph. ii. 2.) They are at present under the wrath of God (Rom. i. 18, 21, 23), while as to their future the sentence is, "Idolaters shall not inherit the kingdom of God." (1 Cor. vi. 9.) They not only stand without (Rev. xxii. 15), but "shall have their part in the lake that burns with fire and brimstone, which is the second death." (Rev. xxi. 8.)

SECTION II.—THE HEATHEN CONDEMNED.

But we note, farther, that the Scriptures also represent the heathen as *under the righteous condemnation of God's law.*

If, as we have seen, God's word never views idolatry as a misfortune, but as a crime the most detestable of all, which no circumstances can excuse, and which God's jealousy never spares, then the worship of the heathen is itself sufficient to condemn them. Even if they had all the virtues that respect humanity, this would leave them guilty before God. But to this they have added the most flagitious crimes. Such were often their religious services, but their lives in addition were as constant and as direct violations of the second table of the law as their worship was of the first. "And we are sure that the judgment of God is according to truth against them that commit such things."

But here it is necessary to enquire as to the ground on which the heathen are condemned. It cannot be for the rejection of the gospel. This would be, indeed, the Almighty reaping where he had not sowed, and gathering where he had not strawed. But the principle upon which the Scripture place their condemnation is, that *they disregard a light which they possess and violate a law which they know.* In particular, the Apostle Paul, in the greatest of his epistles, that to the Romans, discusses the whole question in a formal and elaborate manner. His great theme there is, that the gospel is the power of God unto salvation to Jew and Gentile alike, as revealing a righteousness which will avail before God. (chap. i. 16, 17.) But in order to establish this He first shows that both these classes are sinners, and as such condemned. (v. 18.) "The wrath of God is revealed from heaven against all ungodliness and unrighteousness of men," that is, against sin, whether in those forms in which it is against God, directly and solely, or in those in which it also respects our fellow-men. From this principle he proceeds to show the sinfulness and consequent condemnation of the heathen. He commences by representing them as having a revelation of God in nature, but as departing from Him, being unwilling to attend to the light, and their hearts being opposed to his character. (v. 18-21.) "Who hold down the truth through unrighteousness, for that which may be known of God is manifest in them, for God manifested it unto them." The works of creation in all their complicated arrangements manifested the wisdom, power and goodness of the Creator, as well as His existence. "For the invisible things of Him," His existence and attributes, not perceived by the bodily senses "since the creation of the world, are clearly seen, being perceived through the things that are made," that is, through the works of creation which are obvious to our senses, not excluding man in his bodily fabric and sentient spirit, "even His eternal power and divinity."

The apostle adds, "that they may be without excuse; because that knowing God they glorified Him not as God, neither gave thanks; but became vain in their reasonings, and their senseless heart was darkened." Men loved darkness rather than light. From their corrupt hearts they refused to acknowledge God in His true character, or to render that love and gratitude which is His due, and in consequence they lost the light. The eye being evil, the whole body was full of darkness. The light that was in them was darkness, and O, how great was the darkness! At the same time they took credit to themselves for superior wisdom, but thus only plunged into deeper darkness. "Professing themselves to be wise"—and a Chinaman or Hindoo of the present time will vaunt himself of his superior knowledge as loudly as the cultured heathen of the apostle's day—" they became fools and changed the glory of the incorruptible God for the likeness of an image of corruptible man, and of birds, and four-footed animals and creeping things." (v. 22, 23.) But as all this proceeded from a depraved heart, as they restrained, kept back, or as our New Version translates, "held down the truth through unrighteousness," they are without excuse, and under the displeasure of the righteous Lawgiver.

But as the fruit of their idolatry they were found as the heathen are now, living in the foulest immorality. "Wherefore, God gave them up in the lusts of their hearts unto uncleanness, that their bodies should be dishonoured among themselves." (v. 24.) Instead of "living soberly," they "sinned against their own bodies" in every form of sensual impurity, especially in that vice to which Sodom has given its name—a vice practised by Alexander the Great, and by many of those occupying the highest rank and the most esteemed in the Roman State. (v. 24-27.) And equally did they live in violation of every duty owing to their fellow-men. "Because they refused to have God in their knowledge, God gave them up to a reprobate mind, to do those things which are not fitting, being filled with all unrighteousness, wickedness, covetousness, full of envy, murder, strife, deceit, malignity, whisperers, backbiters, hateful to God, insolent, haughty, boastful, inventors of evil things, disobedient to parents, without understanding, covenant breakers." (v. 28-31.) To this black catalogue, he adds a circumstance which filled up the cup of their iniquity. (v. 32.) "Knowing the ordinance of God, that they which practise such things are worthy of death, not only do the same, but also consent with them that practise them." Men do wrong, drawn by desire or inflamed by passion, but to approve of others in the commission of such crimes, manifests an inward delight in evil, which argues the highest degree of depravity.

That the apostle correctly delineates the moral condition of the heathen in his day, has been abundantly shown by the examination of the state of Greek and Roman society, as revealed in their literature and depicted on their remains; and now that 1800 years have elapsed since the words were written, we see that they portray the present state of the whole heathen world, as exactly as they did its condition in the apostle's time. The conclusion is inevitable, according to the principle on which the apostle had started, that they are under the displeasure of the righteous Lawgiver of the universe, "for the wrath of God," the strong repulsion of His holy nature from sin, "is revealed or made known from heaven," whether in the hearts or consciences of men, or by the Spirit of revelation, or by God's judgments in Providence, precursors of the day of final sentence, or in all these ways together, yet at all events certainly and effectively "against all ungodliness and unrighteousness of men." (v. 18.)

That the heathen are thus condemned the apostle unfolds more fully in the second chapter, but in connection with the state of the Jews, that he might show the condition of both as under the sentence of the law, and thus needing the righteousness revealed in the gospel. The latter prided themselves on their privileges, but the apostle argues that these would not save them if they did evil. (v. 2.) "We know that the judgment of God is according to truth against them that practise such things." God was no respecter of persons, and would render to every man according to his works, whether Jew or Gentile. (v. 7-11.)

From this he concludes that both shall be punished, because both have sinned. (v. 12.) "As many as have sinned without law, shall also perish without law." Those who had not the written law and sinned, shall be punished for their sins, but not as if they possessed a revelation. They shall be judged according to the light they had. But, on the other hand, those who enjoyed a written revelation shall be judged by it. "As many as have sinned under law, shall be judged by law." For, he argues, it is not the possession of the law that will save. (v. 13.) "For not the hearers of a law are just before God, but the doers of a law shall be justified." If the possession of a law could save, he goes on to show that the Gentiles also had a law. (v. 14.) "For when the Gentiles, which have no law, do by nature the things of the law, these having no law are a law unto themselves." Though they have not the written law, yet by their acts in harmony with it they manifested the existence in them of a law. Not that they kept it in its entirety. On the contrary, they broke it constantly, as he had shown, and in the most flagrant manner. But in particular acts they showed their knowledge of it, and in the judgment they formed in regard to the character of human deeds they showed that, if they had not the law as originally written, they had it engraven upon their hearts (v. 15), " in that they show the work of the law written on their hearts, their conscience bearing witness therewith, and their thoughts one with another accusing or else excusing them," the tone of the apostle indicating that they would accuse rather than excuse. As he thought of such accusations in this life, his mind rapidly passes on to the day of judgment, when they would be manifested more decisively; and without stopping to indicate by any phrase the course of thought, he adds (v. 16), " in the day when God shall judge the secrets of men, according to my gospel by Jesus Christ."

An examination of the state of the heathen, either in their past history or present condition, amply confirms the statements of the apostle regarding their knowledge of moral duty, and also as to their sense of guilt. Nothing has been more thoroughly established in the present day both by the intercourse of missionaries with races under every form of idolatry, and by the investigations of the learned into the literature of the more cultured among them, than that they everywhere show the law written on their hearts, and that no opposing influences can entirely obliterate it. The Hindoos, for example, adopted Pantheism, which lays the axe at the root of all moral obligation, but it could not quench conscience within them. Even their mediæval writings, which are full of childish absurdities and worse, and which in their religious conceptions contrast so remarkably with those of an older age, yet oftentimes exhibit the duty of man to man with clearness, force, and even beauty. The golden rule itself may be found in them. In practice the morality of the people was not high, but such writings show that there still remained in them a light which man had not kindled, a knowledge of right and wrong which was not the result of education, but had been implanted by the Creator. Call it natural conscience, moral sense, natural religion, there it is in every man, inextinguishable for ever. The most savage tribe to whom the missionary goes is found not without this law written on their hearts. The light that is in them may be obscured, but experience shows that it is still there and may revive at a touch. They at least see and condemn in others the evil that they practise themselves; and the missionary has not yet found a tribe in which the heart does not respond to the teaching of right. Thus in no circumstances is man found without a witness for God and a law unto himself.

But such investigations have equally shown that this light is powerless to guide the conduct of men in opposition to their passions and the natural depravity of the heart. Hence, as certainly as they have this law, they do not keep it; as certainly as they have this light, they walk contrary to it. Men are universally sinners, and by their own consciences stand condemned.

The charge of guilt the apostle brings home to the Jew with great force from chapter ii. 17 to chapter iii. 9, showing that both stand in the same position. (ver. 10.) "We before laid to the charge of both Jews and Greeks that they are all under sin." On the principle that what the law says, it says to them who are under it, he therefore concludes that all mankind, Jew and Gentile, must stand speechless and without excuse before their great Judge (ver. 19), "that every mouth may be stopped and all the world may be brought under the judgment of God." None possessing the revealed law have done what it commands, none under the natural law have fulfilled its requirements. Then the revealed law proclaims, "Cursed is every one that continueth not in all things written in the book of the law to do them." The law in the heart of man says that he who does wrong, he who does not do what he knows to be right, deserves punishment, and everywhere among the heathen is found the sense of ill-desert which responds to the justice of the sentence.

Of course, the punishment of those possessing fewer

privileges will be proportionally light. "He that knew not, and did commit things worthy of death, shall be beaten with few stripes. For unto whomsoever much is given, of him shall be much required." Hence it shall be more tolerable for Tyre and Sidon, yea, even for Sodom and Gomorrha, in the day of judgment, than for those who misimprove gospel privileges. (Matt. xi. 22, 24.) The heathen will not have to answer for rejecting the Saviour. This is a sin with which not even demons are chargeable. But let us not think lightly of their doom. "Is it little to endure 'the few stripes?' Is it scarcely to be deprecated that they shall only be banished from the Divine presence, shut out of heaven, and disqualified eternally for the ends of their existence? Though but one chain, is it therefore easy? Can the mildest flame be endured? How dark must be the nearest line of the outer darkness!"*

But, it may be asked, would a heathen be accepted if he kept the law which he was to himself—who followed the light which he possessed? We answer, certainly, "the doers of the law are justified." But worshipping idols was not keeping the law, neither was vice. And where is the man to be found who has met its requirements? The apostle speaks of what would be in such a case, but only to show that no man can claim to be in such a position. The conclusion, then, of his whole argument is that both sections

---

* Dr. R. W. Hamilton.

of mankind have broken God's law, as they respectively possessed it, and therefore "by the works of the law shall *no flesh be justified in His sight.*" (ver. 20.)

But we must look at the subject in another light. The disobedience of the heathen proceeds from an evil heart: "The carnal mind is enmity against God." Men thus defiled are entirely opposed to His holiness, and regard His service or communion with Him with utter dislike. But "without holiness no man shall see the Lord." Could the law be set aside, God's judgment-seat overturned, and the sinner received without a justifying righteousness, the truth, "Except a man be born again, he cannot enter into the kingdom of God," would still stand as a flaming sword to keep the way of the tree of life. But alas! taking the heathen as we find them, where do they give any indication of their being "renewed in the spirit of their mind," and thus being fitted for dwelling in the presence of infinite purity? Surely, if heaven is a place of perfect holiness, then the heathen, with the character which we have found them everywhere to possess, are unfitted for it and could find no enjoyment in it. We pronounce it too pure for men upright in business, and for women amiable in all domestic relations, unless regenerated; and it is simply absurd to suppose that men, living as the heathen do in the unrestrained indulgence of the evil passions of humanity, can be partakers of its happiness. The Scripture has assigned them their place: "Without are the dogs, and the sorcerers, and the fornicators, and the murderers, and the idolaters, and every one that loveth and maketh a lie."

But as the Spirit of God works in some unknown way on the minds of infants and idiots, implanting in them the germ which only requires favouring circumstances to cause it to bring forth all the fruits of Christian life and character, may it not be that He will work in the same way in the minds of the heathen? We certainly do not deny the possibility of this, and we would not relinquish the hope that there are instances in which He does so. But upon this little can be built. The analogy fails. Infants and idiots are not responsible agents. Adults among the heathen are. They have done wrong, and they are condemned by the law of God and their own consciences. Then, if the Spirit does work savingly in such, it must be by making them like Christ. We need not say that if persons manifesting such a character can be shown in heathenism, most cordially every Christian heart would bound to embrace them. But, again, we are compelled to ask where are they to be found? Do missionaries tell us of their meeting men ignorant of the Bible, whose hearts are directed to a pure God, who hate sin, and die in triumph? The cases where there is even the appearance of anything of the kind are so rare and doubtful, while the mass are found wedded to their corruptions, and even manifest intense hostility to the gospel as soon as it is seen to interfere with their beloved sins, that they scarcely deserve consideration in our estimate of the condition of the heathen, or of our duty to them.

Thus, as the apostle says, "the Scripture hath concluded," or shut up together, "all under sin, that the promise by faith of Jesus Christ might be given to them that believe." Thus the heathen, guilty, depraved and wretched, are at the same time left hopeless and helpless, except as the gospel comes bringing near a righteousness which avails before God, and carrying with it a power that can transform the most depraved into His image. Hence the conclusion of the apostle, "I am not ashamed of the gospel; for it is the power of God unto salvation to every one that believeth; to the Jew first and also to the Greek. For therein is revealed a righteousness by faith unto faith. For the wrath of God is revealed from heaven against all unrighteousness and ungodliness of men who hold down the truth in unrighteousness." (Rom. i. 17, 18.)

SECTION III.—NO REMEDY BUT THE GOSPEL.

But we must further notice that there is *no other remedy*.

Here we would emphasize the fact that in vain do we look for any healing element in heathenism itself. Everywhere it appears not only without recuperative force, but constantly becoming worse. Among nations refined and intellectual, as well as among savage tribes, we find those who have turned from the worship of the one living and true God wandering farther from Him—becoming more senseless in their worship and viler in their conduct. At times, indeed, as the evils of society became overwhelming, there have arisen men of higher moral tone than the mass, who have attempted to stem the torrent of corruption. But the result has been only to show the feebleness of all the devices of human thought and natural instincts to resist the tide of human passions. The current, partially arrested, soon swept away all barriers thus erected, and rushed onward with increasing volume, or if diverted, found new channels, into which it poured in deeper and broader streams.

In this view we come into collision with a form of the philosophy, so-called, of the day. The advocates of the development hypothesis set out with the idea that, instead of man being created in the image of God, and thus from his beginning possessed of a rational and moral nature, distinguishing him from the brutes, he was derived by evolution from them. In accordance with this theory, they find in the various systems of heathen worship different steps in the development of the religious instinct in man—in his upward progress from the period when he is supposed to have been as atheistic as his nearest progenitors, the man-monkeys, now are, till he arrived at pure monotheism, which they are pleased to allow is the highest form of religious development the world has yet seen. They even profess to trace the steps by which he ascended. They suppose that from pure Atheism he passed to what is called Fetichism, in which reverence is paid to material objects of various kinds, in which some supernatural power is supposed to reside; and thence to Shamanism, where worship is rendered to various spirits, generally of evil, and whose power is in some measure at the disposal of Shamans or sacred men. The next stage was to idolatry proper, in which these beings are represented in material forms, the product of human art, to which religious homage is paid, and so on up to pure monotheism.

It is not too much to say of this scheme, that it is a figment of the imagination. Without referring to its opposition to Scripture, it is contradicted by all the facts of the case, as these are made known by the past history of mankind and by the present condition of races under every system of idolatry. These show, conclusively, that except as nations have been influenced by the revelations of God made in the land of Judea, their progress in religion, both as to its doctrine and practice, has been downward. The religion of the leading peoples still in heathenism, as well as of the cultured nations of antiquity, can be traced back for thousands of years, and the changes through which they have passed noted with more or less exactness; but every examination of the subject only shows more conclusively the comparative purity of the original religious systems from which they sprung, and the mighty contrast which these present to their present degraded forms. Egypt, Chaldea, India, China, as well as Greece and Rome, all show records, exhibiting the state of society among them at a very early period; but all historians are struck with the fact, that in every such case the nearer we go to the fountain-head, the more we find men in their religion following a comparatively pure monotheism.

Even where people have only tradition as to their past, what light it gives only shows the same process of degradation. Without attaching weight to the dreams of a golden age, found among most nations, and making due allowance for the spirit of praising past time, so common among men, even savage tribes can look back to a time when this or the other of their worst evil customs did not exist, and trace their introduction and spread.

Nor does an examination of heathenism anywhere at the present day, except as it is acted on by forces external to itself, show an example of a nation rising to a truer conception of God or a purer moral condition. Not a missionary that has ever gone on his errand of love to the heathen has ever found a tribe that was of itself making progress in religion—not a traveller who has dwelt among a people in unmixed heathenism sufficiently long to fully understand their social condition, but is obliged to report that heathenism has no recuperative force, as the Scripture expresses it, is "without strength;" while the selfish trader and the materialistic philosopher are sometimes the loudest in proclaiming heathen tribes, not only non-progressive, but incapable of improvement.

But what may be accomplished by culture and

civilization. These have had the opportunity of testing their power, both in ancient and modern times, only to show their utter inadequacy to regenerate man. All the culture of the Greeks and Romans left their morals unimproved, and China, India, Paris, in modern times, show the same results. Indeed, a modern philosophic author, writing the "history of culture," declares vauntingly that "times of higher culture-flourish are always times of deep immorality." He adds that the "so-called corruption of morals stands in direct proportion to the increase of civilization, and is positively no retrogression, but a quite natural phase of development." *

But the attempt to transport to heathen lands even the civilization which has grown up under Christianity, without Christian teaching, instead of availing for their spiritual elevation, will only add a new element of power to the evils already working among them. It is unnecessary to refer to the demoralization and destruction of rude and barbarous tribes by their intercourse with white men. But take the most intelligent heathen nation we can find, and try to elevate them by giving them even the best material and mental cultivation which Christian lands can supply, apart from the gospel of Christ, and the result is not only failure, but disaster. A missionary, whose description of the immorality of Japan we have quoted, adds:

---

* Von Hellwald, quoted by Warneck in "Modern Missions and Culture."

"For this frightful state of matters civilization can provide no remedy. We have forced our civilization upon the Japanese, and though reluctant to receive it at first, they are now embracing it with feverish eagerness. But civilization has wrought no improvements on the morals of the people. Perhaps, on the whole, it has deteriorated them. It has shaken the influence of the native religions, diminished respect for mere authority, loosened the old bonds which bound men together. Japan has been suddenly cut loose from her ancient moorings, and sent adrift without compass or pilot on an unknown and shoreless sea. The crisis is a grave one, and if it is to be safely passed special efforts must be made to meet it by every Church labouring in Japan." Similar has been the experience of other nations.

Yes, the gospel of Christ is the only remedy for the spiritual wants of man. "In none other is there salvation, for neither is there any other name under heaven that is given among men wherein we must be saved." The experience of the centuries of heathenism only shows humanity, like the woman in the Gospels, as having "spent all its living upon the physicians, and could not be healed of any." But "seeing that in the wisdom of God the world through its wisdom knew not God, it is God's good pleasure through the foolishness of the preaching to save them that believe." "We preach Christ crucified . . . unto them that are called both Jews and Greeks, Christ is the power of God and the wisdom of God." The command, "Go ye into all the world and preach the gospel to every creature," assumes that Gentiles and Jews are alike perishing. God thus proclaims their need and their only relief at the same time that He sets before us our duty. " Whosoever, then, shall call upon the name of the Lord shall be saved. How, then, shall they call on Him on whom they have not believed ? And how shall they hear without a preacher ? And how shall they preach except they be sent ?"

PART III.

THE DUTY OF THE CHURCH TO SUPPLY THE GOSPEL TO THE HEATHEN.

"I am a debtor both to the Greek and to the Barbarians."—Romans i. 14.

THE DUTY OF THE CHURCH TO SUPPLY THE GOSPEL TO THE HEATHEN.

CHAPTER I.

THE GROUND OF MISSIONARY OBLIGATION THE COMMAND OF CHRIST.

"According to the COMMANDMENT OF THE EVERLASTING GOD, is made known to all nations for the obedience of faith."—Rom. xvi. 26.

SECTION I.—THE COMMAND STATED AND ILLUSTRATED.

"Look to your marching orders: preach the gospel to every creature," is the language in which the Duke of Wellington, when in India, is said to have replied to a chaplain who was maintaining the uselessness of missions to the Hindoos. His common sense and his devotion to duty led him to apply to the service of God that principle of implicit obedience, which is often found absolutely necessary in human undertakings requiring the united efforts of bodies of men. In such cases, while the responsibility for the orders given rests upon those in command, the business of those "under authority" is not to raise any question as to the end contemplated, the wisdom of the means employed, or the likelihood of success, but only to discharge faithfully the duty assigned them.

> "Theirs not to make reply,
> Theirs not to reason why,
> Theirs but to do and die."

This principle carried out in human affairs may sometimes degrade men into acting the part of mere machines. It may render them the passive instruments of wrong-doing. It may thus become a power for evil, the lives of brave men being sacrificed to incapacity, or the interests of communities crushed under the heel of tyranny. Yet scarcely any great work can be accomplished without in some measure acting upon it, and it has called forth some of the noblest examples of self-denying discharge of duty the world has ever seen.

A similar spirit of obedience to the Captain of our salvation is required of every soldier of the cross. It is the test which He has Himself laid down, by which His followers are to be distinguished. "Ye are my friends if ye do whatsoever I command you." As the essence of sin is ignoring and contravening the will of God, so the essence of piety consists in seeking to know and spiritually performing what He requires. Thus the inquiry of Saul at his conversion, "Lord, what wilt Thou have me to do," while a representative experience of the soul returning to God, embodies a principle covering the whole range of human duty, and exemplified to a greater or less degree in every Christian life.

Upon the same basis we place the obligation resting on the Church to engage in missions to the heathen. We know that the service of God in this or any other department is the noblest in which rational beings can be engaged—we know that the ends contemplated are the grandest which infinite love and wisdom have combined to effect—as to the means employed, we need not fear being called to act on a command which "some one has blundered," and as to the issue we may rest assured that ultimate failure is impossible. But our action in the missionary cause, or in any other department of God's service, is not to be grounded on considerations of this kind. The great principle by which we are to be actuated in this, as in every act of human life, is subjection to the will of the Lord. That being ascertained, it only remains for us to say, "All that the Lord hath said we will do and be obedient."

On this subject, however, we need be in no doubt as to what He would have us do. He has not left us to gather His mind by inferences drawn by a studious comparison of one passage with another. He has delivered His command in the plainest terms, and in circumstances the best fitted to render it impressive. When He had by His sufferings unto death purged our sins, and risen in triumph over His foes, He, during forty days, appeared unto His disciples, and spake of the things pertaining to His kingdom; but just before His departure He delivered to them His final command, which is given to us in different forms by the first three evangelists. In Matthew it is given as follows (chap. xxviii. 18-25): "All authority hath been given unto Me in heaven and on earth. Go ye, therefore, and make disciples of all the nations, baptizing them into the name of the Father, and of the Son, and of the Holy Ghost: teaching them to observe all things whatsoever I commanded you: and, lo, I am with you alway, even unto the end of the world."

By Mark it is expressed thus (chap. xvi. 15, 16):

"Go ye into all the world and preach the gospel to the whole creation. He that believeth and is baptized shall be saved; but he that disbelieveth shall be condemned."

Luke thus records His words (chap. xxiv. 46-49):

"Thus it is written that the Christ should suffer and rise again from the dead the third day; and that repentance and remission of sins should be preached in His name unto all the nations, beginning from Jerusalem. Ye are witnesses of these things. And, behold, I send forth the promise of my Father upon you; but tarry ye in the city until ye be clothed with power from on high."

To these we may add the words given by Luke (Acts i. 8), as spoken by our Lord at His last interview with His disciples, and when just ascending into heaven. "Ye shall receive power when the Holy Ghost is come upon you, and ye shall be my witnesses, both in Jerusalem and in all Judea and Samaria, and unto the uttermost part of the earth."

A full exposition of these passages is not necessary for our present object, nor need we dwell upon the differences between them; it is enough for our present purpose to observe their main purport. Obviously the intention of the whole is, to lay a command upon those to whom the words were addressed, to carry the gospel to every part of the habitable earth and to every tribe of men. For fifteen centuries the prophets had confined their ministrations almost exclusively to one people. One land was chosen as the scene of the special manifestations of Jehovah, and one nation selected as the depositary of divine truth. "To them pertained the adoption, and the glory and the covenants, and the giving of the law and the service of God, and the promises." But now the middle wall of partition is broken down, and there is to be no distinction among the nations as to their right to enjoy the gospel. The whole earth is to be hallowed ground, and Christ's disciples are constituted His ambassadors to make known His salvation to every people upon its surface. If the command was to "begin from Jerusalem," this merely expressed the order of procedure. God was pleased that the first offer should be made to His ancient covenant people; but this was not because they stood upon a different footing from others in the commission. On the contrary, the very terms in which the charge was given imply that it was made to them as one of the "all nations" to whom the apostles were sent.

Let us notice, in passing, the goodness manifested in this commission. As for fifteen centuries He had left the Gentiles to wander in darkness, and none could impugn His righteousness; so, still, He was not bound to bestow upon any people the means of life, and He might have separated some portions of the earth, and forbidden His messengers to visit them. He might have glorified His justice by dooming some of the nations to extinction, as He did the Canaanites, and none could have arraigned His procedure, while holy beings would have sung, "Just and true are all Thy ways, Thou King of saints." But instead of this He has looked in mercy upon all nations, and has laid upon His Church the charge of seeking their salvation, making no exceptions in regard to any on account of their degrading ignorance, their low intellectual capacity, or the polluting and cruel nature of their idolatries.

Not only so, He has commanded her to *go to them*. She is not to wait for invitations, nor be satisfied with responding to the cry of perishing nations when it reaches her ears. They are sunk in spiritual slumber, insensible of their need, and, under the influence of their carnal minds, will seek no change. And the responsibility is laid upon her of going to them with the message of life. The command binds her by the authority of her great Head, and leaves her no option. It requires her to carry the means of grace to every part of the world, irrespective of soil or climate, and to preach Christ on continent and island, on mountain and plain, by river and sea, amid Arctic snows and Equatorial heats. It lays upon her the obligation to hold forth the word of life to every tribe of earth, without distinction of race, colour, or condition, and to tell her message to Greek and Barbarian, to the rudest savage and the cultured philosopher—to the acute Hindoo and the degraded Hollander—to bond and free—in short, to man wherever found—in the kraal of the Hottentot and the snow hut of the Esquimo— in the wigwam of the wandering American Indian and the tent of the Arab—in the zenanas of India and the crowded cities of China. All alike are the objects of the commission, and only circumstances, which at present render it beyond her power fully to accomplish the work, can relieve her from the responsibility of doing so, and nothing can exempt her, or any of her members, from doing at least what is in their power toward the object.

Such, then, is "the law of the house." "The commandment of our ascended Saviour," says James Montgomery, "is the Magna Charta of salvation to all the fallen race of man. It has never been restricted or repealed, and it never will be till all things are fulfilled which are written in the law of Moses, and in the prophets, and in the Psalms concerning Him." Upon this and this alone we base the obligation of missions to the heathen, whether for the confounding of adversaries or moving the consciences of the friends of Christ. We ground it not upon the state of the heathen, though that may well move our sympathy, for they were as ignorant, as wicked and as wretched before the command was given as they are since. Nor do we place it upon the success of missions in the past, or the prospect of a greater in the future, though these are well fitted to encourage us in the work, for " though Israel be not gathered, yet shall the Son of man be glorious." But we place it simply, according to the apostle, upon '*the commandment of the everlasting God.*"

Our adversaries may tell us that the heathen are better as they are for this life, and their perdition an imagination of Church bigotry. They may argue that our labours will be fruitless, that this tribe is too low intellectually to be taught, and that too savage to be reclaimed; that in vain we assail systems venerable from antiquity, rooted in the prejudice of millions, and firmly established by the prescription of ages. We are prepared to meet such arguments at the proper time and place, but the question at present is of the divine law, and were such allegations as true as we believe them to be false, still obedience to the Master leaves us no option as to the course we should pursue. It calls us to go because He commands—whithersoever He commands, to the uttermost part of the earth—to deliver the message which He has entrusted to us, repentance and remission of sins—to all to whom He commands us, even to every creature under heaven—and to know neither pause nor rest till that end be accomplished.

Upon this high principle, too, we seek to move the

consciences of the lovers of the Saviour. We draw arguments, motives and encouragements from reason and history, from the state of the Church and the world, from Providence and Redemption; but these are all subsidiary, and only valuable as they serve to impress more deeply on our mind the work of Christian missions, as duty devolving on us by our subjection to our ascended Lord. There is much in such appeals to excite the emotions, but all impressions produced in this way are too weak to form a motive power in the heart sufficient to maintain true Christian zeal on behalf of missions to the heathen. Only that absorbing sense of obligation to the Master, which, proceeding from a heart inspired with love to Him, constrains men to say, "All that the Lord hath said we will do and be obedient," will call forth the self-denial and the sacrifices necessary for the work, and maintain the patience required during the weary days of sowing and waiting till the harvest comes.

"We want a motive power sufficient to impel disciples always with uniform force, which will survive romance, which will outlive excitement, which burns steadily in the absence of outward encouragement and glows in a blast of persecution; such a motive as, in its intense and imperishable influence on the conscience and heart of a Christian, shall be irrespective at once of his past history, of any peculiarities in his position, and of his interpretation of prophecy.

"We have it; we have it in the clear law of Christ and His constant love." *

---

* Dr. Herdman's address at Mildmay Conference.

SECTION II.—THE COMMAND ENFORCED BY THE CIRCUMSTANCES IN WHICH IT WAS GIVEN.

But, further, the command was given in a manner and under circumstances to render it solemn and impressive. It was uttered by our Lord soon after His crucifixion, when the scenes of His life and death were fresh in the minds of His disciples, and while they were rejoicing in His resurrection presence with them. Behind Him were the cross, the shame, and the spitting; before Him were the glory and the crown. He had finished the work given Him to do. He had won salvation for men, and as He mounts the throne of universal empire, He contemplates the world lying in the wicked one, in its evangelization He sees the joy set before Him, for which He had endured the cross, and the same love which brought Him from the bosom of the Father to the sorrows of Gethsemane and Calvary, burning within Him, leads Him, before leaving the world, to make provision that all lands should enjoy the blessings purchased with His blood, by giving to His disciples the commission to carry to them the means of life.

This charge He delivers in the way best fitted to impress it upon their minds. He carefully instructs them as to its meaning. "Then opened He their understanding that they might understand the Scriptures." He exhibits it while as a new injunction, yet as the fulfilment of ancient prophecy. "Thus it is written." He repeats it in different forms and at successive interviews. The most formal statement of it, that given by Matthew, was uttered in circumstances well fitted to imprint it in indelible lines upon their hearts and memories. It was delivered on the "mountain in Galilee, where Jesus had appointed them" (chap. xxviii. 16), at the solemn gathering of the whole body of His disciples, to which in His lifetime He had directed their expectations (chap. xxvi. 32), to which the angel who announced His resurrection summoned them (chap. xxviii. 7, Mark xvi. 7), and at which our Lord Himself, on His appearance, commanded their attendance, with special promise of meeting with them (Matt. xxviii. 10)—doubtless the same meeting of which Paul speaks, at which were present more than five hundred brethren—all the believers in Him at that time on earth who could attend.

Mountains have been chosen by God as the scene of some of the grandest manifestations of Himself that He has made to men; but perhaps no hill of earth, not Sinai itself even when God came down upon it to legislate for His creatures, ever exhibited a scene of greater moral grandeur than did that mountain in Galilee, when the risen Saviour, about to ascend to His Father, stood upon it in the midst of that company of humble men and women and committed to them the charge of carrying the glad tidings to the ends of the earth. In that interview were bound up the hopes of the world, and the everlasting destinies of the human family.

The command was prefaced by the assertion of

His universal sovereignty, which He speaks of as already enjoyed, from His being just about to enter upon it. "All authority is given to Me in heaven," where "angels, principalities, and powers are made subject to Him," and especially where He will obtain power to send down the Spirit, in all His saving energy, "and on earth," "over all flesh, that He should give eternal life to as many as the Father has given Him," and over nature, that all her powers may serve Him and His people. He is now to be exalted as Head over all things to His body, the Church, with everything necessary for her support, extension, and prosperity at His command. Whatever the obstacle before His messengers, whatever the difficulties they may have to encounter, whatever dangers may beset their path, they are encouraged to go forward, knowing that all events are under His control. But at the same time, this authority demands their implicit obedience. He who hung upon the cross, now from His throne claims their services. And at the same time it is the pledge of success. The five hundred brethren, five hundred times multiplied, were of themselves powerless to convert a single soul, but through His might even the dry bones "shall stand up upon their feet, an exceeding great army."

Then how grand the commission. The King of Persia would send his couriers to the one hundred and twenty-seven provinces of his empire, but this Son of man, sends His agents to every part of the habitable globe—not to demand the unwilling service of subject races, or to gather the treasures of the people for the support of tyranny, but to bring a willing people to yield their best fruits to Him, and to pour heavenly blessings into the lap of every human family. And He follows it with the promise of His continued presence. " Lo, I am with you alway, even to the end of the world," by My grace to uphold you, My comforts to cheer you, My Providence to protect you and to prepare the way before you, and by My Spirit to render your message effectual.

And then in the moment of parting He renews His charge, giving it thus all the force of a parting word and a last injunction. As He stood on the Mount of Olives, about to ascend to the glory prepared for Him, it is His last concern as He leaves His disciples. He meets all difficulties as to their weakness by the promise that they should receive power by the Holy Ghost coming upon them. And while the transforming power of His ascension glory was working in Him, He for the last time repeats His charge, to testify to His salvation "to the uttermost part of the earth." "And when He had spoken these things, while they beheld, He was taken up; and a cloud received Him out of their sight." (Acts i. 8, 9.) His last act was blessing and dismissing them to their work; His last words thrilled with love and zeal for the salvation of a perishing world; His last look glowed with the intensity of His interest in the object, and the last impression on their minds was, that He had committed a trust to them for the world.

And they stood there as representatives of the whole Church. This is evident from the promise: "Lo, I am with you alway, even unto the end of the world." Unless they had been immortal, they could not have enjoyed His promised presence during these successive ages, or have reached every creature. It must therefore have been intended for the Church in its succession, "till the last syllable of recorded time." So that we should feel this charge with its mighty requirements, its glorious authority and its gracious promise, to be as truly addressed to us as it was to the first disciples, and as fresh in its obligations to-day as when it first sounded in their ears.

"If Jesus should stand again on the Mount of Olives, and summon us before Him, as He summoned the disciples of His personal ministry, and the apostles of His extraordinary call; if He should collect you and me, and all the officers and all the people of His Church on earth, what think you would be the language in which He would address us? It would be an august spectacle—a solemn and awful scene. The words that He would speak would pierce our souls, and stir the very depths of our being. They could never be effaced from the memory. We should think of them by day and dream of them by night; and the most anxious cares of business would never drown them. The voice would ring in our ears wherever we went, at home, in the market, by the wayside, as we lay down and as we rose up. It would be an era in our history never to be forgotten. Is it presumption to imagine what these words would be?.. There is no need for any exercise of fancy. He was once present with His collected Church, and He did give her a parting mandate: "Go ye into all the world." *

---

* Dr. Thornwell's sermon before the General Assembly of the Presbyterian Church of the United States, 1856.

CHAPTER II.

THE COMMAND IN RELATION TO THE PREVIOUS DISPENSATIONS OF GOD'S PROVIDENCE AND GRACE.

"The times of this ignorance God winked at, but now commandeth all men everywhere to repent."—Acts xvii. 30.

FULLY, however, to appreciate this command, we must consider the circumstances in which it was given, in connection with the previous arrangements of God's providence and grace.

SECTION I.—THE COMMAND DISTINGUISHES THE OLD TESTAMENT FROM THE NEW.

In the first place, we notice that this command marks *one leading point of contrast in the position and duties of the Church under the New Testament and under the Old.*

The latter was indeed a light shining in a dark place. Israel was set in the midst of the nations. Situated at the head of the Mediterranean, and in the very centre of the great historical kingdoms of antiquity, it spoke by its history and institutions to the surrounding nations, proclaiming the power of the one living and true God, and directing their hopes to the coming seed of Abraham. From the time of the coming out of Egypt, " they had heard that the Lord was among this people." (Numbers xiv. 14.) But yet no commission was then given to the Church to evangelize any neighbouring people, nor did her constitution make any provision for such an enterprise.

True religion is the same under all dispensations, and the spirit of missions must have marked the pious heart in all ages. Hence the Gentile proselyte was welcomed to the covenant blessings of the seed of Abraham. The language of Moses to Hobab, " Come with us and we will do thee good," expressed the spirit in which his system opened its portals to receive any who renounced idolatry, even to its highest honours. Of the recorded ancestresses of the Saviour, three—Tamar, Rahab, and Ruth—were not of Israel. The two former were of the race of Canaan, doomed to extinction for their abominable crimes. The latter was of the Moabites—a people excluded from the congregation of the Lord (Deut. xxiii. 3)—yet how cordially was she received to " the God of Israel, under whose wings she had come to trust." The faithfulness of such converts is even recorded in a way to put to shame the chosen seed. Ittai, the Gittite, adheres to David, when all Israel went after Absalom, and how strong the faith and how dauntless the courage with which Ebedmelech, the Ethiopian, delivered Jeremiah when his countrymen sought his life. Doubtless, too, many brought into connection with Israel by servitude or otherwise, were incorporated with the people of God, and became partakers of their privileges—abundantly sufficient to show that then as ever "God was no respecter of persons, but that in every nation he that feareth God and worketh righteousness was accepted of Him." Thus the Jewish Church was as open to the admission of the Gentiles as the circumstances in which she was placed would admit. Still, with one partial exception, during the whole period of her history, no mission was sent to any heathen country, nor did she put forth any direct efforts for their conversion to God.

This was not that they did not need salvation. The dark places of the earth were then as now, "full of the habitations of cruelty." Human sacrifices polluted their altars, and the rites of Moloch were as bloody as those of Jagannath. The temples of the Phœnician Astarte, or the Babylonish Mylitta, were scenes of as foul services as can be witnessed at any idol shrine in India at the present day. Nor was God indifferent or unconcerned. He was ever the jealous God, who would "not give His glory to another, nor His praise to graven images." Still He gave no call to His Church to interpose for the instruction of the heathen around, but "suffered all nations to walk in their ways."

Even when the national glory culminated in the reigns of David and Solomon, these pious princes, with all their zeal, undertook no mission for the conversion of the heathen. This was not from want of means. He who could collect for the building of the temple a hundred thousand talents of gold, and a thousand thousand talents of silver, and brass and iron without weight, and besides could give of "his own proper good" three thousand talents of gold, and seven thousand talents of refined silver to the house of the Lord, or his son, who "made silver to be as the stones in the streets of Jerusalem," certainly did not want for financial resources to carry on a mission in any heathen territory. Nor were the heathen inaccessible. The neighbouring tribes were subjugated, so that the dominion of these kings extended from the river of Egypt to the Euphrates, while Tyre, and the great kingdoms on the banks of the Nile and the Tigris were in friendly relations, and men came from the uttermost parts of the earth to hear the wisdom of Solomon. Nor was it from want of men. David apportioned 38,000 Levites for the service of the house of God, and need not have wanted agents for a missionary expedition to any of the surrounding countries. Nor was it from want of faith and zeal. David, as the type of Christ, could say, "The zeal of the Lord's house hath eaten me up." The men who "through faith subdued kingdoms, wrought righteousness, stopped the mouths of lions, quenched the violence of fire," would have needed no more faith to have gone on a mission to proclaim the vanity of idols, and the authority of the one living and true God, to any heathen tribe, had the Lord so commanded. This would have involved no more danger, and called for no more sacrifices than Micaiah's confronting Ahab, or

Jeremiah's warning the Jews of their sins, or Daniel's going to the den of lions. Yet no prophet entered Babylon to announce the supremacy of Jehovah, or proclaimed to the inhabitants of Thebes the vanity of the gods of Egypt. The worshippers of Moloch in Ammon or of Chemosh in Moab were undisturbed in their bloody rites by any messengers of the Most High calling them to repentance, while no attempt was made to supplant the foul rites of Astarte in Phœnicia by the ritual of a purer worship. And this for the simple reason that God had not given to His Church any command, or any authority to do so.

Doubtless, the events of Israel's history were the means of shedding some light into the surrounding darkness. The Queen of Sheba represents a widespread feeling, when she described the temple of Solomon as "a house exceeding magnifical of fame and glory throughout all countries." The navy of Hiram must have carried back to Tyre intelligence of a religion whose principles struck at the foundation of their idolatry. The ambassadors of the King of Babylon came to the court of Hezekiah, to "enquire of the wonder done in the land." (2 Chron. xxxii. 31.) Naaman, who had received such evidence of the power of Jehovah as to profess his conviction that "there was no God save in Israel" (2 Kings v. 15), must have made known this truth to the court of Syria. In these and other ways some knowledge of the true religion must have been diffused which would exert a corrective influence upon heathenism.

The sages who travelled through many lands in search of wisdom, could not have been altogether ignorant of that land where one God without material form was worshipped, and must have learned something of the purer religious teaching there enjoyed. The influence thus exerted by the people of Israel upon ancient heathenism we believe to have been more extensive than is generally supposed, but it was almost entirely the silent influence of their position and institutions. As a people they engaged in no active propagandism or any direct efforts to communicate to other nations the light and the blessings they were enjoying.

Even when from and after the captivity to Babylon the Jews were scattered among the nations, carrying everywhere some knowledge of the true God, drawing some from the worship of idols, and preparing the way for the dissemination of the truth in the fulness of time, they engaged, properly speaking, in no mission to the people among whom they dwelt. Ezekiel, though he prophesied to the exiles by the river of Chebar, had no message for the heathen around him; and even Daniel, though preserving his faith entire and his conduct pure in Babylon, made no effort to convert the king and his court to the worship of Jehovah.

One notable exception there was to this in their history. Jonah was commissioned to call the Ninevites to repentance, and the main lesson of his mission was God's grace to men of all nations. The history in which it is recorded presents the narrow views and exclusive feelings of the Israelitish people, who so far lost sight of the ultimate purpose of their mission as for all nations, as to look for vengeance upon the heathen powers around them. So strong were such feelings even in the prophet that he shrank from a mission to a heathen city, because he believed that from the abounding mercy of God it might issue in their repentance and acceptance with Him (Jonah iv. 2); and he was only excited to anger when God on their repentance turned from the vengeance He had threatened, as if such a proceeding were an injury to God's chosen people. But this only led the All-merciful to teach him more impressively, by direct inspiration, as well as by the monsters and storms of the deep and the fragile plants of the earth, that He is no respecter of persons, affording at the same time to the Church of that era a prelude of that brighter day in the future, when "repentance and remission of sins should be preached unto all the nations."

But this was an isolated phenomenon in the Divine arrangements under that dispensation. It was a singular episode in the history of the Jewish Church—a sort of meteoric brightness flashing across her sky. The fact remains that on the whole she was not a missionary institute. And why? Because she had no command from her king to engage in any undertaking of that nature. Her position was conservative. Like the British squares at Waterloo, it was enough for her during many trying hours to maintain her position, till the time should come when she should receive the signal from her Divine commander to advance to the conquest of the earth.

Even during our Lord's ministry on earth that time had not arrived. He "was not sent but to the lost sheep of the house of Israel." When He commissioned the seventy, it was to "every city and place whither He Himself would come." And when He sent forth the apostles on a preparatory mission, it was under the injunction, "Go ye not into the way of the Gentiles, and into any city of the Samaritans enter ye not."

But with His resurrection came "the fulness of times." The treasure so carefully preserved in the casket of the Mosaic institutions is brought forth and entrusted to the Church, not as hitherto, to be laid up and faithfully guarded, but to be distributed among the destitute of every land. The servants are now to go forth to the highways and hedges of heathenism to announce that "all things are ready," and to gather the outcasts to the marriage feast of the King's Son.

SECTION II.—THE COMMAND THE OUTCOME OF ALL GOD'S PURPOSES PREVIOUSLY REVEALED.

Secondly, we must consider this command, as the *outcome of all the purposes of God, revealed and prefigured under preparatory dispensations.*

The Scripture, foreseeing that God would justify the heathen through faith, preached before the gospel unto Abraham, saying: "In thee shall all nations be blessed." (Gal. iii. 8.) Even the first promise in Eden, of the seed of the woman bruising the head of the serpent, was general; but when God called Abraham from among the people of the earth, it was with a more distinct promise of universal blessing: "In thee shall all families of the earth be blessed" (Gen. xii. 3), and again: "In thy seed shall all the nations of the earth be blessed." (Gen. xii. 18.) That the seed referred to is Christ, and that the blessing denotes the spiritual privileges secured in Him, is fully argued by the apostle Paul (see particularly Gal. iii. and Rom. iv.), and the very point of the promise is, that these were for all nations.

At a later period, when His descendants had increased to a multitude, and the darkness of heathenism had grown denser, God saw fit to separate them as a nation to Himself, and to establish among them a special economy of religious ordinances, in order to preserve them from being absorbed by other nations, thus constituting them the keepers of His oracles, the depositaries of His successive relations to man. But this did not alter His design, as revealed in the promise to Abraham: "This I say, that the covenant, which was confirmed before of God in Christ, the law, which was four hundred and thirty years after, cannot disannul, that it should make the promise of none effect." (Gal. iii. 17.) The promise of the Messiah was independent of the Mosaic ordinances, neither was salvation bound up with them. There is only one reference to Christ in the record of the Jewish economy, and that is one that implied that He should abolish the Levitical institutions. It is the promise of a prophet like unto Moses (Deut. xviii. 18)—one who would occupy a position similar to his in establishing a new dispensation, and to whom all should be subject. "Wherefore, then, serveth the law?" might the Jew ask. "It was added," the apostle replies, "because of transgressions, till the seed (viz., Christ) should come, to whom the promise" of blessing to all nations "was made." It was the casket in which for a time the treasure was preserved till the time should arrive appointed for its distribution.*

When revelation advanced, and in the elevation of David to the throne of Israel, the Messiah was typified as a king, this only leads the Psalmist to picture in more glowing terms His ministry as for all nations. In the second Psalm He is represented as crowned by His Divine Father king in Zion, and the heavenly voice proclaims: "Ask of Me and I shall give thee the heathen for thine inheritance, and the uttermost parts of the earth for thy possession." In the twenty-second, after picturing the priestly sufferings of the Messiah, he describes the result in its widespread influence: "All ends of the earth shall remember and turn unto the Lord, and all the kindreds of the nations shall worship before Thee." (v. 27). And the seventy-second, while describing His benignant and glorious administration, marks His dominion as extending

---

* Throughout this discussion, I must acknowledge my indebtedness to Somerville's lectures on Missions and Evangelism.

"from sea to sea, and from the river, even to the ends of the earth." "Yea, all kings shall fall down before Him, all nations shall serve Him." (v. 8, 11.)

In the declining years of the kingdom, when the earthly expectations which might have been formed of the fulfilment of these promises in their national glory under the house of David, were being extinguished in the weakness and decay of their monarchy, the hearts of the prophets were only the more earnestly directed to the future, and under the inspiration of the Spirit of God their language becomes more fervid and glowing, and they ransack nature to find images to picture the glorious state of things under the coming One, who was to rule all nations. "It is a light thing that thou shouldst be My servant to raise up the tribes of Jacob, and to restore the preserved of Israel. I will also give thee for a light to the Gentiles, that thou mayest be My salvation to the ends of the earth." (Isa. xlix. 10.)

We cannot notice all the passages of this kind, but must refer to two or three from the prophecies of Isaiah. He commences his book with threatenings of judgment upon Israel for their apostasy, but in the midst of these there bursts upon him a vision of the coming glory. "The mountain of the Lord's house shall be established in the top of the mountains, and shall be exalted above the hills, and all nations shall flow unto it. And many people shall go and say, Come ye and let us go up to the mountain of the Lord, to the house of the God of Jacob." (chap. ii. 2, 3.)

Then follow denunciations of judgment upon the hostile nations around, but in the midst of these woes he describes the righteous ruler, of the stem of Jesse, under whose reign peace and righteousness should prevail among all the inhabitants of the world, "the earth being full of the knowledge of the Lord as the waters cover the sea," and who should "stand up as an ensign of the people, and to which the Gentiles should seek." (chap. xi. 4, 9, 10.) Again, amid such calamities, he breaks in with the joyful tidings of spiritual blessings for all nations: "In this mountain shall the Lord of hosts make unto all people a feast of fat things, of wines on the lees, of fat things full of marrow, of wines on the lees well refined. And He will destroy in this mountain the face of the covering cast over all people, and the vail that is spread over all nations." (chap. xxv. 6, 7.)

In his later prophecies he delineates more minutely the coming Saviour and the blessings to be enjoyed under Him, but in whatever office he represents Him, it is as exercising it for all nations. Thus, in the forty-second chapter, he says: "Behold my servant, whom I uphold; mine elect, in whom my soul delighteth; I have put my spirit upon him. He shall not cry, nor lift up, nor cause his voice to be heard in the streets," etc.—a passage which Matthew applies to his personal teaching; but it is added, "He shall bring forth judgment to the Gentiles. He shall not fail nor be discouraged till he have set judgment in the earth, and the isles shall wait for his law." "I will give thee for a covenant of the people, a light of the Gentiles, to open the blind eyes," etc. (chap. xlii. 1-7.) Then in the fifty-second and fifty-third chapters, when he pictures Him as the suffering and atoning Messiah, it is for all nations. "His visage was so marred more than any man, and his form more than the sons of men. So shall he sprinkle many nations." If he is wounded for our transgressions and bruised for our iniquities, then God will "divide him a portion with the great," and the Church is summoned to prepare to receive a large accession from the converted Gentiles. "Enlarge the place of thy tent, and let them stretch forth the curtains of thine habitations; spare not, lengthen thy cords, strengthen thy stakes; for thou shalt break forth on thy right hand and on the left; and thy seed shall inherit the Gentiles." (chap. liv. 2, 3.)

And just as he pictures the Church as blessed and glorified of her Lord, he represents her as exercising an attractive influence upon other nations, or, in other words, assuming a missionary character. "Behold thou shalt call a nation that thou knowest not, and nations that know not thee shall run unto thee because of the Lord thy God, and for the Holy One of Israel; for He hath glorified thee." (chap. lv. 5.) If the Church is called to "arise and shine for her light is come, and the glory of the Lord is risen upon her," then "the Gentiles shall come to her light, and kings to the brightness of her rising;" and the prophet calls her to rejoice in the glorious vision of nations coming and bringing all their treasures to her feet. "Lift up thine eyes round about, and see: all they gather themselves together, they shall come to thee: thy sons shall come from far, and thy daughters shall be nursed at thy side,—the abundance of the sea shall be converted unto thee, the forces of the Gentiles shall come unto thee,—all they from Sheba shall come: they shall bring gold and incense; and they shall show forth the praises of the Lord." (chap. lx. 1-7.) Thus will be realized the prayer of the Psalmist, "God be merciful unto us and bless us; and cause His face to shine upon us; that thy way may be known upon earth, thy saving health among all nations." (Psalm lxvii. 1, 2.)

And passing on to the close of the prophetic canon, we may only notice how the prophets, who ministered to the returning exiles from Babylon, directed their hopes, not so much to any future national elevation, but to the bringing of the Gentiles into subjection to Israel. Thus speaks Zechariah, "And the Lord shall be King over all; in that day shall there be one Lord and His name one," and at the same time he represents all nations as coming to observe the Feast of Tabernacles, glad festival of a redeemed earth. And when the voice of Old Testament prophecy was about to become silent, Malachi, condemning the selfishness and earthliness of the Jews, announces the coming change in the Divine arrangements: "I have no pleasure in you, saith the Lord of hosts, neither will I accept an offering at your hand. For from the rising of the sun even to the going down of the same My name shall be great among the Gentiles; and in every place incense shall be offered unto My name, and a pure offering; for My name shall be great among the heathen, saith the Lord of hosts." (chap. i. 10, 11.)

The Jews, as a people, did not enter into the spirit of these declarations. They expected to continue forever the favourites of heaven; and the promised subjection of the heathen to the Messiah they interpreted literally as their being subjugated and rendered tributary at the feet of Israel. But this exclusiveness, though it might prove ruinous to themselves, and was one cause of their rejection as a people, could not hinder the fulfilment of God's purpose of grace to the Gentiles.

As the time drew near, when the long-expected Messiah was to appear, John the Baptist was raised up to announce His coming, to prepare Israel for it, and finally, when He did appear, to point Him out to God's waiting people. But born as he was of the priestly order, educated as he was in the Levitical law, yet elevated above the exclusiveness of his countrymen by the teaching of the Spirit of God, he announces Him as the great sacrifice, the fulfilment of the Mosaic types, but one whose mission was to have neither local nor national limitation—a Saviour not for Jew alone, but for mankind, not for one land, though it be the glory of all lands, but for the earth. "Behold the Lamb of God, which taketh away the sin of THE WORLD."

When at length the expected child was born in Bethlehem, it was announced from heaven with angelic songs; but while a single messenger commenced the strain, proclaiming the grace which came first to Israel, "Behold I bring you glad tidings of great joy, which shall be to all the people" (viz., Israel), suddenly a whole angelic choir joined in one grand chorus, celebrating the extent of the coming blessings as to every part of earth, "praising God and saying, Glory to God in the highest, and on earth peace, good will toward men." And men under the teaching of God rejoiced in the same hopes. Wise men from distant regions came to offer their adorations at the feet of the infant Redeemer—token of the homage of the Gentiles—and presented their richest offerings—first-fruits of the pure offerings which were to be presented from every hill of earth. At His early presentation before the Lord, the expectant faith of the spiritually-minded of Israel found expression in the inspired utterances of Simeon:

" Now lettest Thou Thy servant depart, O Lord,
According to Thy word, in peace;
For mine eyes have seen Thy salvation,
Which Thou hast prepared before the face of all
    peoples;
A light to lighten the Gentiles,
And the glory of Thy people Israel."
Luke ii. 29-32.

SECTION III.—GOD MADE PREPARATION IN PROVIDENCE THROUGH CENTURIES FOR CARRYING OUT THE COMMAND.

Thirdly. We notice that God *for centuries had been preparing in Providence for the carrying out of this commission.*

Among the ways in which this was done might be mentioned the wide diffusion of the Greek language, from the conquests of Alexander the Great and subsequent events; the extension of the Roman Empire bringing so many of the nations of the known world under one Government, and establishing law and order, thus preparing the way for free intercourse between different countries; and the dispersion of the Jews from and after the captivity to Babylon, as well as the moral and social condition to which the world had been brought through heathenism. The space at our disposal, however, will not permit a full discussion of these topics.

CHAPTER III.

THE COMMAND ILLUSTRATED IN THE TEACHING OF OUR LORD.

"And I, if I be lifted up from the earth, will draw all men unto myself."—John xii. 32.

WE must now consider how *the same principles were manifested in the personal ministry of the Son of God.*

Born under the Mosaic institutions, He became a minister of the circumcision, but this only with a view to the ultimate extension of His salvation to the Gentiles. This was intimated in various ways. When He taught His disciples to pray, in that form of prayer which was to be the guide of the Church's devotion in all her subsequent history, and the expression of her highest religious life, summing up in six or seven petitions the things to be desired of God, three of them, and these the first three, are for the glory of God in the spread of the Gospel, with the whole earth, in opposition to heaven, as the scene of its triumphs: "Hallowed be Thy name, Thy kingdom come, Thy will be done in earth as it is in heaven." (Matt. vi. 9, 10.) In His instructions He taught that, as a Divine cultivator, His "field is the world"—that, as a shepherd, His care was not to be confined to those in the Jewish fold: "Other sheep I have, which are not of this fold: them, also, I must bring." (John x. 16.) He is the "light of the world" (John viii. 12), and when He called His disciples to Him, it was that they might perform the same office. "Ye are the salt of the earth. Ye are the light of the world. A city that is set on an hill cannot be hid." (Matt. v. 13, 14.) His kingdom He likened in its external form to the seed growing to a tree in which the birds of the air found shelter, and in its internal power in human society, as leaven, which from a centre should spread from particle to particle, "till the whole was leavened."

Though His personal ministry was so far confined to the Jews that He might say, "I am not sent but to the lost sheep of the house of Israel," yet in His mission to the Samaritans at an early stage of His ministry, and His visit at a later to the coasts of Tyre and Sidon, with its extension of grace to a woman of the accursed race of Canaan, He gave a foretaste and prelude of the time coming, of which He had on more than one occasion given intimation to His disciples, when "the gospel should be preached to all the world," or, as Mark expresses it, "published unto all the nations." (Matt. xxiv. 14, xxvi. 13; Mark xiii. 10, xiv. 9.) It might be observed, further, that throughout His ministry His gospel from the first had no reference to local or national distinctions, but was proclaimed in terms applicable alike to all mankind. At the outset He announced to a Pharisee, that "God so loved *the world* that *whosoever* believeth in Him should not perish." And this was the spirit of all His preaching. "If *any man* thirst, let him come unto Me and drink." "If *any man* enter in, he shall be saved."

How He contemplated this work appears from the manner in which His spirit was comforted, amid Jewish unbelief, by the faith of the heathen centurion foreshadowing the ingathering of the Gentile nations. "They shall come from the east and from the west, and from the north and from the south, and shall sit down in the kingdom of God." (Luke xiii. 28, 29; see also Matt. viii. 11.) Similar were His feelings when, on going up to the feast at which He was to "finish transgression and make an end of sin," certain Greeks applied for an interview with Him. Looking beyond the cross He sees Himself exalted, but, as the result, His ministry no longer limited, and these Greeks the pioneers of the "exceeding great army" which should be enrolled under His banners and render Him their faithful service. If death is first, it is only the sowing of the seed of an abundant harvest to be gathered from among the Gentiles. "The hour is come that the Son of man should be glorified. Verily, verily, I say unto you, except a grain of wheat fall into the earth and die, it abideth by itself alone, but if it die it beareth much fruit." (John xii. 23, 24.) Then He declares the principle on which He was to act, and applies it to His disciples, unfolding to them the conditions on which alone they would be suitable instruments for extending His kingdom: "He that loveth his life loseth it, and he that hateth his life in this world, shall keep it unto life eternal. If any man serve Me, let him follow Me." (ver. 25, 26.) But as He announces the thought that He must die, His whole soul is pressed down by the view of all that this involved: "Now is my soul troubled." The Evangelist lets us into the depths of His heart, as he gives the words in which He expresses the struggle through which He was passing: " What shall I say, Father save me from this hour." This nature prompted. The desire is addressed to the Father, no doubt hypothetically, like the " if it be possible " of Gethsemane. But then, to save Himself would be the ruin of the world. He has advanced too far to turn back. " But for this cause came I unto this hour." Love triumphs. He represses the voice of nature, and under the Spirit pours forth His filial love in the prayer, "Father, glorify Thy name." "There came, therefore, a voice out of heaven, I have both glorified it," in the Saviour's past ministry to Israel, "and I will glorify it again." That this is to be in His agency for the conversion of the world is evident from our Lord's reply, "Now is the judgment of this world." Now is the time of decision regarding it.* Who shall rule? Satan has long had a usurped sway over it, and men were his

---

* The word translated "judgment" means, according to the Lexicons, "issue, decision." It is used to denote the crisis or turning-point in disease, and we think might be so rendered here, which, in fact, would only be transferring the word.

willing subjects. Now the question is to be decided whose it shall be. The issue is not doubtful. The world is not to be Satan's. " Now shall the prince of this world be cast out;" his right to rule will be gone, and, in due time, his kingdom *in fact* will be overturned. "And I, if I be lifted up from the earth, will draw all men unto Myself." By His sufferings unto death He shall become the heir of all things, all nations come to serve Him and enjoy His blessings, and every foot of earth be given to Him for His inheritance.

So much did this enter into the designs of God, that the Spirit of prophecy compelled the high-priest, though a man wicked enough to recommend the murder of our Saviour from expediency to testify to it. "Being high-priest that year, he prophesied that Jesus should die for that nation, and not for that nation only, but that also He should gather together in one the children of God that are scattered abroad." (John xi. 52.)

Finally, when our Lord was concluding His ministry with His disciples in His high-priestly prayer, He starts from His vocation to glorify the Father, and for this end receiving sovereignty over mankind. "Father, glorify the Son, that the Son may glorify Thee; even as Thou gavest Him authority over all flesh, that whatsoever Thou hast given Him to them He should give eternal life." Then He pours out His soul in supplications to God on behalf of His apostles as His agents, and for those who should believe on Him through their word, but all in order to the ultimate object of His mediation on earth, the conversion of the world. "That they may all be one, as Thou, Father, art in Me, and I in Thee, that they may also be one in us: and that the world may believe that Thou hast sent Me." (John xvii. 1, 2, 21, 23.)

In short, if He was made under the Mosaic law, and lived the life of a good son of Abraham, if He observed its ordinances and fulfilled all its requirements, it was that He might obtain salvation for all nations. "For I say that Christ hath been made a minister of the circumcision for the truth of God, that He might confirm the promises given unto the fathers, and that the Gentiles might glorify God for His mercy, as it is written:

"Therefore will I give praise unto Thee among the
    Gentiles,
  And sing unto Thy name.
And again he saith:
  Rejoice, ye Gentiles, with His people.
And again:
  Praise the Lord, all ye Gentiles,
  And let all the people praise Him.
And again Isaiah saith:
  There shall be the root of Jesse,
  And He that riseth to rule over the Gentiles,
  On Him shall the Gentiles hope."
                        Rom. xv. 8-12.

And now when the salvation is achieved—when the

feast is provided, the oxen and fatlings killed and all things ready—when God is glorified, His law magnified and sin atoned for, then He appears not as the minister of the circumcision, but as the Saviour of the world. Even when the kingdom of God could only be said to be near at hand, His ministry was limited, but now when it is fully come, its gates are thrown open to the whole human race, and the "mystery of Christ, which in other generations was not made known unto the sons of men, as it hath now been revealed unto His apostles and prophets in the Spirit, *to wit*, that the Gentiles are fellow-heirs and fellow-members of the body, and fellow-partakers of the promise in Christ Jesus through the gospel" (Eph. iii. 4, 6), found expression in this commission to His disciples, "Go ye into all the world, and preach the gospel to every creature."

CHAPTER IV.

THE COMMAND AS CARRIED INTO EXECUTION IN THE PRIMITIVE CHURCH.

"They went forth and preached everywhere, the Lord working with them, and confirming the word by the signs that followed."
—Mark xvi. 20.

SECTION I.—PREPARATION FOR IT AND COMMENCEMENT ON THE DAY OF PENTECOST.

IN considering the execution of this command in the primitive Church, our attention must first be directed to the *preparation for carrying on the work and the commencement of it on the day of Pentecost.*

The disciples were commanded "to tarry in Jerusalem, till they should be clothed with power from on high." In many respects they were unfitted for the work entrusted to them, but the promise was, "Ye shall receive power when the Holy Ghost is come upon you." The promise was fulfilled on the day of Pentecost. It was the first day of the week, and the disciples were assembled with one accord, waiting doubtless in prayer for the fulfilment of the Divine word, when "suddenly there came from heaven a sound, as of the rushing of a mighty wind, and it filled all the house where they were sitting. And there appeared unto them tongues parting asunder, like as of fire; and it sat upon each one of them. And they were all filled with the Holy Ghost, and began to speak with other tongues, as the Spirit gave them utterance." (Acts ii. 2-4.)

In this we may notice, *first, the emblem in which the Spirit descended.* Formerly He appeared as a dove, and He was frequently promised in the Old Testament under the emblem of the rain and the dew, but now He came in the form of tongues, doubtless to indicate the proclamation of His gospel to all nations and languages. It was significant that this took place when representatives of many lands were present. And when those sojourners, who had come from the banks of the Euphrates and the Nile, and even from far-off Rome, heard in their own tongue the wonderful works of God, it was an evidence that this was a gift not for the Jews, but for mankind, and afforded a gladsome prelude of the time when all nations and languages should do honour to the Messiah.

Secondly, We notice *how the agents were by this effusion of the Spirit qualified for the work.* Up till this time their views of the Saviour's work were crude and earthly. On the morning of His ascension they had asked, "Lord, wilt thou, at this time, restore the kingdom unto Israel." But now entirely purged of such carnal notions, Peter and his companions could preach Him in His true kingly authority, "made Lord and Christ," "exalted a Prince and a Saviour, to dispense repentance and remission of sins." But recently they had stumbled at the idea of His dying, now His cross is their glory and their hope, the central theme of their preaching. Thus had the Spirit led them into all truth.

Not less did He give them the moral and spiritual qualifications requisite for their work. Before this they had shown the spirit of selfishness and worldly ambition, and when the time of trial came their courage had failed. But now they were prepared to speak Christ's name before kings and not to be ashamed; now they were ready to sacrifice every personal interest, to go to prison and to death for the name of Jesus. But these were only the first-fruits of the rich harvest of gifts to be bestowed for the building up of His Church till she arrive at her final glory. (Eph. iv. 8-13.)

Thirdly, In the loud sound as of the rushing of a mighty wind, there was *the emblem of power*. Accordingly, with the preaching of the Word, the Spirit worked so mightily that three thousand, some of whom Peter charges with being implicated in the Saviour's death, were savingly drawn to Him. In this there was shown an agency sufficient to convert the world to God, and it was but the commencement of an effusion which was to continue till the second coming of the Son of man. (Joel ii. 28-31; Acts ii. 18-20.)

It is important here to notice this event as connected with the time of giving the commission. Without the Spirit not a soul could be converted.

But the bestowment of such a blessing upon the sinful could only be through the atonement of the Saviour. The scanty drops that had fallen during previous ages were in anticipation of this; and, not until He had actually purged our sins, did it accord with the Divine wisdom that the Spirit should be poured out in the copious showers of gospel times. Previously it was said, "the Spirit was not yet given, for Jesus was not yet glorified," and until He was given such a commission would have been useless. But with His exaltation came the power of dispensing the Spirit, and with this came the commission: " Go, disciple all the nations."

Then, farther, the Spirit works by means, but the great means of saving sinners is the Word of Truth, especially the great truth of Christ crucified. It is as lifted up on the cross that He draws all men to Him, and only when He had actually died was the instrument provided by which the Spirit works in the hearts of men.

At the same time, the Mosaic institutions, having served their purpose, were to pass away. They were suited only to a dispensation local and limited, and their continuance would have confined the Church within narrow bounds. But now they had fulfilled their purpose and were no longer binding. They were, indeed, suffered to stand for a time during the transition period, but in a short time the whole would be overturned in the destruction of Jerusalem and the temple. But, in the meantime, the New Testament

Church would be established, with institutions simple and easy to be observed by the poorest as the richest, adapted to every land and every climate, and thus according with a commission which was wide as the worl

SECTION II.—STEPS BY WHICH THE CHURCH WAS LED TO ENGAGE FULLY IN THE WORK OF EVANGELIZING THE HEATHEN.

Secondly. We must next notice *the various steps by which the Church was led to enter fully upon the work of carrying out the command.*

The apostles, as commanded, began at Jerusalem. We might have thought that, with such glad tidings of great joy to communicate, they would have been in haste to finish their work there and set out on their mission to the world. The Jews were slow to admit the broad truth, that the Gentiles should share with them, on equal terms, the blessings of God's covenant. It was contrary to all their former modes of thought and feeling. Even the apostles retained some of this prejudice, and God by His providence and by direct revelation would constrain them to obey the Divine command. Persecution arose, compelling the disciples to go abroad, and thus tending to the extension of Christ's kingdom, as wherever they went they preached the gospel, though still only to the Jews. But God was to teach them, in a still more impressive manner, the duty of extending the blessings of salvation to the Gentiles. By a vision to Peter, three times repeated, He taught him that there was no distinction of Jew and Gentile as to gospel privilege. At the same time, Cornelius, a representative heathen, was visited by an angel with a message to send for Peter, and the Spirit of God directly commanded the latter to comply with the invitation. When he did, the Lord gave testimony to His work by the effusion of the Holy Ghost on those who heard. By these wondrous signs did God set His seal to the first preaching of the gospel to the Gentiles.

But a more public preaching to them followed. Some of the Jewish preachers, scattered by persecution, came to Antioch, the ancient capital of the Greek kingdom of Syria—a city supposed to have contained at this time half a million of inhabitants, a great centre of trade, and the third city in the Roman Empire, but now selected by God as the point from which the gospel was to be diffused among the nations. There "they spake unto the Greeks also, preaching the Lord Jesus." And the Lord marked their work with the seal of His special approbation. "The hand of the Lord was with them, and a great number believed and turned unto the Lord." Intelligence of this was brought to Jerusalem, when the Church there deputed Barnabas to visit Antioch, who, when he came, rejoiced at what he saw of God's work. Through his labours much people were added to the Lord; but, finding the work increasing, he obtained the assistance of Paul, and together they laboured there for a whole year, "and taught much people." Here they formed a true "Christian Church," consisting of Jews and converts direct from heathenism, and received that name in which all the world shall yet glory.

A third step was taken by the call of Barnabas and Paul to the work of missions to the heathen, and their being sent forth by the Church there to the undertaking. The narrative is as follows (Acts xiii. 1-3): "Now there were at Antioch, in the Church that was there, prophets and teachers; as Barnabas, and Simeon that is called Niger, and Lucius of Cyrene, and Manaen, the foster-brother of Herod the tetrarch, and Saul. And as they ministered to the Lord and fasted, the Holy Ghost said, Separate me Barnabas and Saul for the work whereunto I have called them. Then when they had fasted and prayed, and laid their hands on them, they sent them away." This is a most instructive passage, and, the event recorded being what may be considered the commencement of organized effort to send Christianity to the heathen, must rank among the most important in the world's history. We cannot, however, do more than just note two or three points which it presents, as bearing upon our present object. In the first place, it is to be noticed that it was when the Church through its officers, and doubtless the whole body acting in conjunction with them, was filled with earnest, spiritual desires, and in prayer and humiliation were waiting upon God, seeking something higher and better than they had yet attained, that the call came to engage in this work.

Their prayers may have had reference to the spread of the gospel, and, if so, the answer was direct. But at all events it shows that as a Church rises in spirituality so will she become missionary in her character, and when God would bless His people, it is by calling them to give His gospel to the destitute.

A second noteworthy point is the place assigned to the Church in the transaction. Four years before, on his conversion, Paul had received intimation from the Saviour of his call to go to the Gentiles (Acts xxvi. 18), and the intimation was repeated when he went to Jerusalem (Acts xxii. 21); and his calling is here announced as of the Holy Ghost, yet the call was not to be carried out except through the agency of the Church at Antioch. Paul and Barnabas would not go; the Holy Ghost would not send them, except as commissioned by her. This conveys a most valuable lesson. The work of converting the heathen is not the work of missionaries. It is the work of the Church. They must be called internally by the Spirit of God to it, but they go as sent by her. Upon her the charge is laid of sending the gospel abroad. Those employed in the work are but her agents, and upon each member of the body rests a share of the responsibility of the undertaking.

And the last point we shall notice is, that they were commanded to engage in this work, while not only the larger portion of their province, but the majority of the inhabitants of their own city were in heathen darkness. Of the half million of the population of

Antioch at that time, the Christians must have been but a handful. When so much was to be done at home, were they to spend their strength in efforts abroad? When the labourers were so few, were they to send some away, even such men as Paul and Barnabas? Here comes up the question, which is ever rising before the Church, Is it her duty to engage in missions to the heathen, while there are so many at home in a state of comparative heathenism? To answer no, is simply to set human wisdom against the Divine will and Divine wisdom. God teaches her by this example, that as she labours for the destitute abroad, just so will her home work prosper: "There is that scattereth and yet increaseth, and there is that withholdeth more than is meet, but it tendeth to poverty." We believe it is a rule of the Divine procedure, to which the history of the Church shows no exception, that just as any portion of the body in the spirit of the command, "Freely ye have received, freely give," engages in missions to the heathen, just so will she be blessed in all her home undertakings. Christ then calls His Church, with all that her hands may find to do at her door, at the same time to do her part for the salvation of the "world lying in the wicked one." If any section be weak and struggling with difficulties, just the more need has she to engage in this work. She needs all the self-denial she can get, and nothing will so tend to raise her members above all earthly selfishness as efforts for foreign missions made in the spirit of genuine sacrifice. For her own best interests, therefore, she cannot afford to dispense with such.

SECTION III.—PROSECUTION OF THE WORK.

Thirdly, we must notice *the execution of the work thus begun of carrying the gospel to the heathen.*

The whole of the remaining part of the Acts of the Apostles is a record of the work of missions, with Antioch as the centre, and Paul, as the representative apostle of the Gentiles, the central figure, while the thirteen epistles, acknowledged to be his, all bear upon the work, either in its first stage of preaching Christ to the heathen, or in its second of building up churches gathered from among the Gentiles, in the knowledge and holiness of the gospel. Indeed, some of these can scarcely be understood or appreciated, except by our being acquainted with the state of matters in churches gathered from among the heathen in our day. For our present purpose, we can only note some leading points.

First, we notice that the great means which the apostle employed was the preaching of Christ crucified. We have some of his discourses, and we have declarations as to the matter and manner of his preaching, but all show that his great theme was salvation through the sufferings unto death of the Son of God. "We preach Christ crucified, unto the Jews a stumbling-block, and unto the Greeks foolishness; but unto them which are called both Jews and Greeks,

Christ the power of God and the wisdom of God." (1 Cor. i. 22-24.) If he ever tried a discussion of a different kind, it was when, contending with the philosophers of Athens, he delivered his magnificent discourse on Mars' Hill, in which he treats of some of the high themes which have engaged the thoughts of men; but nowhere that we read of did his labours prove of so little avail. And it does seem significant that immediately after, when coming to Corinth, depressed in spirit, he determined to know nothing among her licentious crowds, or before her philosophers and rhetoricians, but Christ and Him crucified, the result was the gathering of much people to the Lord. So the missionary now must go to the heathen, not to civilize the savage or to discuss philosophy with the cultured, but to preach salvation to sinners through the great atonement, and the message is found, as in the apostle's day, "the power of God and the wisdom of God."

Then, secondly, what a model of missionary zeal and activity—what an example of self-denial and patient endurance—have we in the life of the great apostle of the Gentiles. On this what can we add to what he has himself said (2 Cor. xi. 23-33): O, that a double portion of his Spirit rested upon all the ministers and missionaries of our day.

Our subject does not lead us to consider any questions connected with the management of missions to the heathen, or we might find ample materials for the direction of churches and missionaries, in carrying on the work, in what might be called the missionary tactics of the apostle. One point, however, is so prominent, and bears so directly upon our object, that we must notice it, though briefly. We cannot but observe how he chose central places as the scene of his labours, and how rapidly he passed from one place to another. The Acts of the Apostles, from the beginning of the 13th chapter to the end, is just the record of his progress in planting the gospel in one leading city of the Roman Empire after another. Antioch in Pisidia, Philippi, Thessalonica, Athens, Corinth, Ephesus, mark the principal stages in his career, till he reached the point at which he had long aimed, of preaching Christ in imperial Rome itself. Had the Church in modern times acted on the same principle the world would be nearer evangelization than it is.

Then, as we see, the apostle does not wait in one place till the whole population is brought under Christian influence. Long before that is the case, he feels that "he has no more place in these parts," and presses forward to the regions beyond, suggesting two thoughts, first, the truth to which we have already adverted, that the work at home does not warrant the Church in neglecting her duty to the world abroad; and, secondly, the important principle that each Church, as organized, is to become a self-extending missionary centre, from which "the word of the Lord should sound out in the region around." For nothing was the primitive Church more remarkable than for the missionary zeal which glowed in the feeblest churches and the poorest of their members. Even Gibbon specially notes this among his five causes of the success of Christianity. Obloquy, loss of goods, stripes, imprisonment, death, were cheerfully endured that Christ's name might be known by the perishing. The similar spirit manifested in our day by the converts from heathenism is one of the most hopeful signs of the future. The Church is a living thing, and each part animated by the Spirit of life, growing and extending, she will fill the whole earth.

Finally, we must notice the success which attended the labours of the apostolic men of those days. We need not dwell on this, but the fact that the gospel showed itself in their hands the power of God to men of every class—to the self-righteous Pharisee, to the philosophic Greek, to the rude barbarian, to the drunkards and licentious of Corinth, to the lordly Roman—is our encouragement that it will be equally successful among all ranks and races of men in our day. "The weapons of our warfare are not carnal, but mighty through God to the pulling down of strongholds."

CHAPTER V.

PRESENT DUTY OF THE CHURCH TO THE HEATHEN.

"Lord, what wilt thou have me to do?"—Acts ix. 6.

SECTION I.—SPECIAL CLAIMS OF MISSIONS TO THE HEATHEN.

THE question, then, of evangelizing the heathen, is not submitted to us as one on which we are to sit in judgment, or about which we are asked our opinion. It comes to us simply as one of obedience to the Redeemer. "The world lies in the wicked one," and our great commander summons His soldiers to assault the strongholds of the enemy, and to deliver his miserable captives. Mankind are perishing in sin and misery, and the Divine Saviour puts into the hands of His Church the bread and water of life, to carry to them that they may live and not die. The only question with us is, Will we be obedient to His command, will we be faithful to His charge?

Of course, the commission is not limited to the heathen. As we have said, it includes all mankind, or all of them who are living without God, whether under this or any other form of religion, or under no form at all. But that the heathen are specially referred to is evident. When it was issued, "the nations," to all of whom the apostles were to go, were, in the current language of the Jews, simply the heathen. And when we consider the religious condition of mankind at the present day, we will see that if the world is ever to be converted to Christ, the evangelization of the heathen is the great work devolving on the Christian Church.

Look, first, at their numbers. Eight hundred millions of our race are still worshipping other gods and dishonouring the Most High by services which are as a smoke in His nostrils. Mohammedanism, which is next to heathenism the most powerful foe of Christianity, does not count one-fifth that number of souls. Heathenism then, it must be apparent, taking this view alone, is the very stronghold of the enemy, which will require the whole energies of the Church to effect its subjugation under the sway of Emmanuel.

Then consider the nature of the system. It is that which presents the most direct antagonism to the Creator, which contravenes all His rights. All other systems, even Mohammedanism, do acknowledge Him and profess in some form or other to serve Him. But heathenism denies Him altogether, rejects all His claims, and substitutes for His worship every observance that can most dishonour Him. In its nature, then, it is the great foe of Christianity.

But farther, if we consider the condition of the heathen—their ignorance, their social degradation, their polluting vices, their misery—where does the world show a case presenting such a call for that which alone can heal the spiritual maladies of man? There are ignorance and vice in Christian lands. There are spots where lust and crime appear in frightful forms and to an appalling extent. But the worst of Christendom is not as low as heathenism at its best. We do not need to say that nowhere, even in nominally Christian lands, can there be found the ferocious cruelty, the disgusting cannibalism, the unnatural lust, which rule among savage tribes, whether in Asia, Africa, or the South Seas. But take heathenism at its best estate. Look at it as exhibited among the Hindoos—a people of the same original stock with ourselves, of warm affections, and naturally fervid religious temperament. At the present moment, indeed, through the influence of missionaries and the power of the British Government, some of their worst observances in the name of religion, Sutteeism, Thuggism, and human sacrifices, have been suppressed. Yet still of much of their religious services it is a shame even to speak, and we have seen how far their moral condition is below that of any even nominally Christian people.

Then no part of Christian lands can compare with heathen countries in its destitution of religious ordinances. In the former the Bible is everywhere accessible, and generally ministers so numerous that we can scarcely enter a rural hamlet without finding rival sects contending for the privilege of ministering the gospel to its inhabitants. How different the state of any heathen country. No land has received more missionary labour in modern times than India. Yet, even there, millions on millions have never seen the face of a missionary, or heard the name which is above every name, and are dying, with reason to say, "No man cared for our soul."

If this is the case with India, what of other heathen countries? Of the eighteen provinces of China, eight, each of which numbers its population by tens of millions, are without a single resident missionary, and others have only two or three. Hundreds of towns and villages were never trod by the foot of a herald of the cross, while, taking the whole population, there is not one missionary for one and a half millions of inhabitants. This is about equal to two for the population of the Dominion of Canada. And vast regions of Asia and Africa are equally destitute.

If we believe, then, that faith cometh by hearing, and hearing by the Word of God, does not the condition of the heathen pre-eminently call for the efforts of the Church to send to them the gospel of salvation? And when we consider the extent of the field, it is evident that, if they are to hear the word of life, she must put forth effort on a scale far transcending anything she has hitherto done.

But, lastly, we must say that the events of God's providence, at the present time, loudly call for her efforts in this direction. In the carrying out of the commission, He who has put the times and the seasons in His own power, directs His servants as to the particular fields to which, from time to time, they should direct their energies. (See particularly Acts xvi. 6-10.) And we humbly conceive that, in the present day, His finger is clearly pointing His Church to the heathen world as the great field for her evangelistic efforts. Why did He give India to England? France, Portugal, Holland, Denmark, all sought the magnificent prize, but God in His providence said, in a voice which all nations might hear, "No, I give it to England." Did not the whole circumstances say, and did not subsequent events repeat the lesson, sometimes in tones which might startle the deafest ear, that it was in order that she might break down Hindoo and Mohammedan exclusiveness; that, by her strong government, she might afford security for Christian missionaries, and that her people might make known the Saviour to the two hundred millions in heathen darkness thus placed under her sway? Why, in answer to so many prayers, has China been opened to intercourse with the West, but that Christ's Church might go up to possess the land? Why is Japan seeking European civilization, but that with it God's people may make known to her that religion upon which it is based? Why is Africa only now opening to intercourse with the civilized world; and why has the Ruler of the earth, at the same time, given to Britain sole control over her Southern extremity, established her in commanding positions on her East and West coasts, and, while we write, is forcing her, in opposition to the wishes and disinterested counsels of her wisest and best rulers, to retain her hold of Egypt on the North? Why, but that she may keep the door open, especially against Moslem fanaticism, that the armies of the living God may go up over the land, so that "princes may come out of Egypt, and Ethiopia *soon* stretch out her hands unto God."

Then, again, why the immense carrying facilities of the present day, by which the world is becoming one vast neighbourhood? Men may see in this only earthly interests involved. But in the coincidence of this free intercourse of nations, with the awakened zeal of the Church for missions, the wonderful achievements of the press, and the vast preparatory work done by missionaries in providing Bible translations and a Christian literature in the languages of the heathen, we may see that these steamboat and railroad lines are established because the Lord hath need of them, not to fetch earthly treasures from distant regions, but to carry imperishable riches to the destitute nations of the earth, according to His word of old: "Many shall run to and fro upon the earth, and knowledge"—surely the best of all knowledge, the knowledge of God and of the Saviour—"shall be increased."

No other system of error presents such openings as heathenism; no other people without Christ are so accessible as the heathen. Islamism, the next greatest foe of Christianity, is fenced in by adamantine walls. Events have, indeed, given it some rude shocks, and there are indications that the time will come when it will totter to its fall, but that time is not yet. By all that has occurred, a fierce fanaticism has taken a firmer hold of its votaries, and to appearance given it a new lease of power. Up to this time missions among them have been almost fruitless, solely because in their proud self-sufficiency, originating with the founder of the system and strengthened by the teaching and practice of centuries, their minds are blinded, and they have closed eye and ear to the truth as it is in Jesus. The veil is still upon the heart of the Jew, and the superstition and infidelity of Christian lands have deliberately chosen the darkness rather than the light. But the heathen through vast regions are accessible, as they were not when the modern missionary enterprise began. And though the natural heart in them is opposed to the gospel, yet their old systems are shaken, multitudes are losing their faith in them, retaining their sense of needs, which the gospel only can supply. Thus the breaker has gone up, the way of the Lord is prepared, and missions among them are everywhere meeting with a due return. "Say not ye, then, there are yet four months and then cometh harvest; behold I say unto you, Lift up your eyes, and look upon the fields; for they are white already to harvest. And he that reapeth receiveth wages and gathereth fruit unto life eternal."

When the Church resumed in modern times the work of missions among the heathen, various objections were raised. The past history of the enterprise has so thoroughly refuted them that most of them are now scarcely heard. There is one, however, which, though its fallacy has been so often shown in experience, is still found to influence even good men. It is said that there are plenty of heathen at home, and that these should be evangelized before sending the gospel to the heathen abroad. As to this view, we have already shown that it is condemned by the practice of the primitive Church, acting under the inspiration of the Spirit of God. The complete evangelization of Judea was never made a "condition preceding" the carrying the gospel to the heathen beyond. When the Christians were a mere handful of the population of Antioch, they were commanded to set apart two of their ablest teachers for a mission to the Gentiles. Three hundred years later the whole city was not Christian. Should they have waited all that time before sending the gospel abroad? Happily for us, this was not God's plan. Had they acted upon it, Britain, the land of our fathers, might have been still in heathen darkness.

But, further, how does it come that these so-called heathen at home are in their present condition? Is it that the Church has neglected her duty of carrying to them the means of life? Then shame on her; but let her not plead her shameful neglect of duty to the few around her, as a plea for neglecting the Saviour's command in regard to the millions abroad. Or is it that these persons prefer practical atheism to the service of Christ. If so, is the Church to leave the multitudes of heathen to perish because some in Christian lands "hate instruction?"

But we would especially add that the cause of missions at home and abroad is one, and never will a Church find her home-work more thriving than when she looks abroad upon the world in love to souls perishing. Nothing has so awakened the Church to the condition of the degraded in Christian lands, as her engaging in the work of missions to the heathen; and we venture to say that never did a section of His body follow the Master's law in sending the gospel to those in heathen darkness, but she found her interest deepened on behalf of missionary work at home, and the blessing of the Lord resting upon her in all her endeavours for that end. "He that watereth shall be watered also himself." "Give, and it shall be given unto you; good measure, pressed down, and shaken together, and running over, shall men give unto your bosom."

SECTION II.—DUTIES OF ALL CHRISTIANS.

Let us now consider the *particular duties devolving* by Christ's command *upon the members of His Church toward the heathen.*

Here let us have it impressed upon our minds that in the work of saving souls God works by instruments. He might have worked without them, but He has not done so and He never will. He never wrought a miracle to send a Bible to a single tribe, nor will He ever work one to instruct any benighted pagan. In the work of turning the heathen from darkness to light, He has chosen to employ men as "co-workers with Him." This is an honour and a kindness to them. He might have employed angels. Had He done so, how would the heart of a seraph have bounded to receive the command to carry the message of love to the most degraded of earth, and with what rapid wings would He cleave the air to fulfil his commission? But men alone are employed. There is not another agency in the universe, whose office it is to proclaim the gospel; and the heathen will remain unevangelized unless it is done by living men. "How shall they call on Him, whom they have not heard, and how shall they hear without a preacher."

True, the work is the Lord's. We cannot feel this too strongly. Paul plants, Apollos waters, but God giveth the increase. "Thus saith the Lord, Cursed be the man that trusteth in man and maketh flesh his arm." "It is not by might, nor by power, but by my Spirit, saith the Lord." But yet, under certain conditions, He has made the salvation of men dependent on human agency. He has given to His Church all the gifts, and all the means necessary for the work, and with them He has also given her the key by which she may unlock the treasury of omnipotent power, and in prayer bring down the Spirit of all grace. And on her wisdom and devotedness, her labours and sacrifices, her prayers and aspirations, He rests the accomplishment of the work. How solemn the thought that upon us, weak and erring men, it is left to hasten or retard the great enterprise of bringing a lost world back to the service and enjoyment of God.

But, further, we would notice that the command is *personal*. Doubtless it was addressed to the Church as an associated body, but this carries an obligation to every member of it as distinct as if it were addressed to him alone. We cannot escape in the crowd. There will be neither churches nor communities, as such, at the day of judgment. Every man is responsible for himself, every man will be judged alone, and each will receive "according to that *he* hath done."

Whatever, then, others do, each should in this matter hear the Master saying, "What is that to thee? follow thou Me." He is the great missionary who came to seek and to save the lost, and to give His life a ransom for many. To every man who would be His disciple He lays down the terms, that he deny himself, take up his cross and follow Him. For any professed servant of His, then, to labour merely to accumulate wealth, to lie on couches of ease, regardless of the cry of perishing millions, and to do nothing to aid in the conversion of the world, the very object for which the Saviour became obedient unto death, is simply to violate the first condition of discipleship.

Then, does any one ask, "What am I to do?" We answer, as partaker of a full salvation, you are called at once to seek that those around you may enjoy the same blessing. Andrew first findeth his own brother, Peter, and brought him to Jesus. So did Philip with his friend Nathanael. So did the woman of Sychar with the men of her city. And so did the gospel sound out from all the Churches planted by the apostles.

But true piety is expansive. We must not confine our efforts to any mere neighbourhood; we must look around upon the world needing the same salvation which we enjoy, and feel no rest in our spirits while they are without it. Jonathan Edwards thus describes a convert in the revival of his day: "She longed to have the whole world saved; she wanted, as it were, to pull them to her; she could not bear to have one lost." We cannot utter the Lord's prayer, with any appreciation of its meaning, without something of the same spirit.

Hence, a first duty devolving upon all who name the name of Christ is prayer for the conversion of the world. How this moved the souls of good men, even when missions to the heathen were scarcely known, will appear from the language of Richard Baxter, near the close of his life:

"My soul is much more afflicted with the thoughts of the miserable world, and more drawn out in desire of their conversion than heretofore. I was wont to look little further than England in my prayers, as not considering the state of the rest of the world; only I prayed for the Jews—that was almost all. But, now, as I better understand the case of the world, and the method of the Lord's prayer, so there is nothing that lies so heavy upon my heart as the thought of the miserable nations. . . . No part of my prayers is so deeply serious as that for the conversion of the infidel and ungodly world—that God's name may be sanctified, His kingdom come, and His will be done on earth as it is done in heaven."

But prayer and sympathy must prove their sincerity by activity. The command to each is, Go; and it is positive and peremptory. It binds each individual, and if you cannot go in person, you must employ others as your agents. This is the Divine arrangement: "How shall they preach except they be sent?" You are to labour for the Lord in your workshop, or in your fields, or to trade with your merchandize, writing upon it, "Holiness to the Lord;" and, with the money so acquired, employ messengers to do your work among the heathen. Each is bound in his sphere to labour for this end, and to omit doing so is simply a sinful neglect of duty.

What shall we, then, say to the fact, that there are thousands in the Churches of this Dominion, who profess to build all their hopes for eternity on the work of the Redeemer, and to have consecrated themselves and all they possess to His service, who never contribute anything to send the gospel to the nations sitting in darkness: "Curse ye Meroz, saith the angel of the Lord, curse ye bitterly the inhabitants thereof, because they came not to the help of the Lord against the mighty." Ignorance may in part excuse them, but let all take heed how they plead this: "If thou forbear to deliver them that are drawn unto death, and them that are ready to be slain; if thou sayest, behold *we knew it not*, doth not He that pondereth the heart consider, and will He not render unto every one according to his works." Indeed we might well tremble for many professors of Christ's name were it not for "the blood that cleanseth from all sin." But let us all be up and doing, before the Master come and find us sleeping.

> "Oh, Christians, view the day
> Of retribution ! Think how ye will bear,
> From your Redeemer's lips, the fearful words:
> 'Thy brother perishing in his own blood
> Thou sawest.' Thy brother hungered, was athirst,
> Was naked, and thou sawest it. He was sick,
> Thou didst withhold the healing; was in prison
> To vice and ignorance—nor didst thou send
> To set him free ! Oh ere that hour of doom,
> Whence there is no reprieve, brethren, awake
> From this dark dream."

But, perhaps, the responsibility for this state of things may not rest altogether upon the *members* of the Church. With some justice they might, in many instances, say, "No man hath hired us." We loved the Saviour, we desired to do His will, we pitied a lost world, but no opportunity was offered us of aiding in the undertaking. And this leads us to consider the responsibility of the pastor. Surely it is his first duty to arrange that, in some regular and systematic way, each member of his flock, male and female, aye, and each lamb in the fold, may have the privilege of contributing to the work.

But, secondly, he is as much bound to set before them the command of the Master in regard to the perishing as he is to preach faith and repentance. This duty he must exalt to the level of the highest. He must hold up the missionary spirit as essential to the full Christian character, and self-denying efforts to win sinners to Christ as a necessary part of that allegiance we owe to Him; not something we may do, but something we must do if we would have Him recognize us as His. This he must do, if he would be able to say: "I am pure from the blood of all men, for I have not shunned to declare unto you the whole counsel of God."

To promote the object, it is important that the people should have information. For this most of them must depend on the pastor, and he will find it to his own account as well as theirs, to collect and diffuse missionary intelligence among them. Especially for the sake of his own soul, for the sake of his congregation, for the sake of a world perishing, let him seek to catch something of the missionary spirit, as evinced in the conduct of Him who came down to the cross of Calvary and wept over Jerusalem. Let him carry this into all his services, we venture to say especially into his public prayers. When, as the mouth of his people, he addresses the eternal throne, let him wrestle with God for a perishing world; let him carry the hearts of his people to the utmost bounds of the human family; let no Sabbath, no service pass without supplications bearing upon the Saviour's last command, and, while he will be blessed himself, he will be educating them for the highest service, the purest joy, and the most glorious reward of the Redeemer's kingdom.

But then there is also a duty devolving on Churches. In carrying on the work, there is needed the united action of Christians, associated together in communities. In this respect, how far the religious bodies of this Dominion come short of their duty! Whole denominations have no organized system of effort for the salvation of the heathen, and of those engaged in the work, how feeble their efforts compared with what they might do! If we look at the command of our Lord, surely we can never think that any Church is fulfilling the trust committed to her, in merely maintaining the cause of God in lands in which it has been established, perhaps, for centuries! Let none plead their weakness as an excuse for neglecting this duty. They can do something, and they are responsible for their one talent. Let none plead the claims of the work at home. If they want that work to prosper, let them take a broader view of their obligations; let them arise to a higher spirit of self-sacrifice for the perishing around, and assuredly the work of the Lord will prosper in their hand.

This involves the responsibility resting upon some to go in person as missionaries. If the real work which the commission assigns to the Church, is to bring the world to the knowledge of Christ, then the enquiry with each person holding the office of an ambassador of Christ, and of every person looking forward to that position, should be not, are there reasons why I should go abroad? but are there reasons sufficient to indicate the will of the Master, that I must stay at home? In the hour of a nation's trial, when she is assailed by powerful foes, the good soldier does not feel it his ambition to serve on garrison duty, or occupy a comfortable position on the home guard. He fills such a situation if he must. But with him the post of honour is fronting the foe or bearing the hardships of the field. When will a similar spirit animate the soldiers of the cross?

SECTION III.—CONCLUDING APPEAL.

In pressing the claims of this cause we might appeal to commercial men, by showing how missions to the heathen have advanced trade. We might adduce such facts as that every missionary in the South Seas represents an increase of $50,000 a year to British trade; and that the Hawaiian Islands have a foreign commerce of $4,000,000, where before missions began it did not reach $300. We might appeal to the scientist, showing how missionaries to the heathen have done more for the comparative study of languages, for ethnology, for geography, than probably all the learned societies of Britain and America; and how they have contributed largely to the advancement of botany, geology, and kindred sciences. We might appeal to the philanthropist, showing how missions to the heathen have carried all the good of our civilization to those in the lowest barbarism—how vice and slavery, infanticide and polygamy, have fled before them; how they have introduced education in place of stolid ignorance, and comfort instead of want—how they have raised woman to her true dignity, and established a pure family life; how they have planted government and order in the place of the rule of brutal violence, and in every way ameliorated the earthly condition of men.

Such results of missions are not to be overlooked. They show Christianity as having the promise of the life that now is. But they are only collateral advantages of the work. The main object of missions is to bring men back to the knowledge and service of the true God, and His own children are the agents appointed for the work. There may be some who join themselves to a misionary society who have not given themselves to the Lord. Many helped to build the ark, who perished in the flood. Many contributed to the erection of the tabernacle, whose carcases fell in the wilderness. Balaam prophesied of a kingdom which he fought to destroy in its infancy, and Caiaphas foretold an atonement in which he had no part. So men may contribute to send the gospel to others, and themselves go down to the pit. And O! we cannot forbear, in passing, to mark the miserable infatuation of such. In hell the "sorer punishment" is reserved for those who reject Christ.

But to you we turn, ye blood-bought, spirit-born sons of the Most High, ye sworn soldiers of the cross. We appeal to you, by your faithfulness to Him who has committed to you the bread of life, that you might bear it to the perishing, and will in due time come to reckon with you as to the manner in which you have discharged your trust. We appeal to you by your gratitude to Him, who has delivered you from the chains of sin and the condemnation of hell, and made you heirs of the heavenly inheritance, and that at the cost of His own life. He now asks in return that, giving your own heart to Him, you convey the same blessings to others. We appeal to you by your own professed consecration to Him, as redeemed by His blood, and born of His spirit. We appeal to you by the past progress of the work—the many consecrated lives that have been offered in this service, and the two millions of converts from heathenism, dispersed in all parts of the world. We appeal to you in the interests of the Church, which receives its richest blessings as she seeks to bless the perishing. We appeal to you from regard to your own souls, which shall receive the heavenly rains, as you water others, and by the future reward which the Saviour in His grace bestows upon him who turns even one sinner from the error of his ways. We appeal to you by all the voices of God's providence, which are calling His Church to go up to possess the earth, and by all the signs of the times, which indicate the downfall of all systems of error, and the coming of the day when the Kingdom of Christ shall be established on their ruins. We appeal to you by all the promises and the oath of God, by which success is rendered certain. We appeal to you by your zeal for the honour of God, which receives its darkest blots in the lives of the heathen, and is to receive its brightest manifestations in their salvation, when He comes to be glorified in His saints, and admired in all them that believe. We appeal to you by your pity for men, your fellows, of the same family, moved by the same instincts and destined to the same immortality, yet now living without God and dying without hope, and of whose future you tremble to think. We appeal to you to retrieve past neglect. "We are verily guilty concerning our brother." Let such considerations, which might indeed cause the stone to cry out of the wall, and the beam out of the timber to answer it, fill your hearts and cause you to weep day and night over the sorrows and sins of our fallen humanity—let them constrain you to wrestle as in agony for souls perishing, and to live for that for which the Saviour died—to stop at no labour, to spare no sacrifices, that Christ's "name may be known upon earth, His saving health among all nations;" and ten thousand ages hence, redeemed souls from among the heathen will still be rising up to call you blessed.

But let there be no delay. While we linger, souls are perishing. We are apt to feel and act as if those millions of heathen were stationary; but it needs no serious reflection to teach us otherwise—that each day numbers make the fatal plunge into eternity.

> "The time of hope
> And of probation speeds on rapid wings,
> Swift and returnless. What thou hast to do,
> Do with thy might. Haste, lift aloud thy voice
> And publish to the borders of the pit
> The resurrection. Then, when the ransomed come
> With gladness unto Zion, thou shalt joy
> To hear the valleys and the hills break forth
> Before them into singing: Thou shalt join
> The raptured strain, exulting that the Lord
> Jehovah, God Omnipotent, doth reign
> O'er all the earth."

THE END.

BY THE SAME AUTHOR.

MISSIONARY LIFE
AMONG THE CANNIBALS.

BEING THE

LIFE OF THE REV. JOHN GEDDE, D.D.,
(First Missionary to the New Hebridies),

WITH A HISTORY OF THE PRESBYTERIAN MISSION
ON THAT GROUP.

12mo, 512 pp.   PRICE, $1.50.

"We trust that this volume will be very widely circulated. It deserves to be. We are quite sure those who once begin Dr. Patterson's narrative will not read much else till they have finished it, and that they will thereby have their interest in the work of missions to the heathen greatly called forth. . . . We could not think of a better volume to be put into congregational and Sabbath-school libraries than this."—*Canada Presbyterian*, Toronto.

"This is an admirable contribution to Missionary literature. It will stimulate the zeal and inspire the faith of every reader. Dr. Patterson has done his work well."—*Canadian Methodist Magazine*, Toronto.

"We have not space to write a tithe of what we would like to state in reference to Dr. Patterson's 'Life of John Geddie, D.D.' He had a grand subject for his pen. We congratulate the friends of Dr. Geddie, and the church of which he was a Minister, on their ability to secure a biographer so competent for his work."—*Wesleyan*, Halifax, N.S.

"Dr. Patterson's 'Life of Dr. Geddie' is, in many ways, a remarkable book. No missionary library should be without it "—*Catholic Presbyterian*, Edinburgh.

For sale at METHODIST BOOK ROOM, Toronto ; also, by DRYSDALE & Co., Montreal ; JAMES BAIN & SON, and JAMES CAMPBELL & SON, Toronto ; McGREGOR & KNIGHT, Halifax, N.S ; or may be ordered through any bookseller.

NEW BOOKS.

The Life of "Chinese" Gordon, R.E., C.B. With Portrait on the title-page. By CHARLES H. ALLEN, F.R.G.S., Secretary of British and Foreign Anti-Slavery Society. Price, post-free $0 0;

<blockquote>"He got the nickname "Chinese" Gordon from his splendid victories in China, in what is called the Great Tai-Ping Rebellion. . . . Occasionally when the Chinese Officers flinched, he would quietly take one by the arm and lead him into the thickest of the enemy's fire, as coolly as though he were taking him in to dinner. He was the means of saving thousands of lives, but he left China without taking a penny of reward."</blockquote>

"A GREAT BOOK."

The Natural Law in the Spiritual World. By HENRY DRUMMOND, F.R.C.E., F.G.S. 414 pp. New Edition Ready. Price 1 75

<blockquote>"This is every way a remarkable work, worthy of the thoughtful study of all who are interested in the great question now pending as to the relations of natural science to revealed religion. . . A mine of practical and suggestive illustrations."—*Living Church.*</blockquote>

30,000 Thoughts. Being extracts covering a comprehensive circle of Religious and allied topics, gathered from the best available sources of all ages and all schools of thought; with suggestive and seminal headings and homiletical and illuminative framework; the whole arranged upon a scientific basis, with classified and thought-multiplying lists, comparative tables and elaborate indices, alphabetical, topical, textual, and scriptural. Edited by the Revs. CANON H. D. M. SPENCE, M.A., JOSEPH S. EXELL, M.A., CHARLES NEIL, M.A., with an Introduction by the VERY REV. J. S. HOWSON, D.D. 8vo, cloth, 540 pp. Price .. 3 90

Rome in America. By JUSTIN D. FULTON, D.D. With a Portrait and Sketch of the Author. By the REV. R. S. MACARTHUR, D.D., New York. 12mo, cloth. Price .. 0 90

The Dance of Modern Society. By WILLIAM CLEAVER WILKINSON. 12mo, cloth. Price 0 70

Father Lambert's Notes on Ingersoll. Paper, 30 cts.; cloth 0 60

<blockquote>"It is a masterly refutation of Ingersoll. It should be widely circulated."—REV. T. G. WILLIAMS, President Montreal Conference.</blockquote>

SALVATION ARMY SERMON BOOKS:

Aggressive Christianity. 12mo, cloth, 60 cts.; paper 0 35
Godliness. By MRS. CATHARINE BOOTH, with Introduction by DANIEL STEELE, D.D. 12mo, cloth, 60 cts.; paper .. 0 35

WILLIAM BRIGGS,
78 & 80 King Street East, Toronto.

C. W. COATES, Montreal, Que.   S. F. HUESTIS, Halifax, N.S.

BOOKS

PUBLISHED BY

WILLIAM BRIGGS,

78 & 80 KING STREET EAST,

TORONTO.

By the Rev. John Lathern.

The Macedonian Cry. A Voice from the Lands of Brahma and Buddha, Africa and Isles of the Sea, and A Plea for Missions. 12mo, cloth $0 70

The Hon. Judge Wilmot, late Lieut.-Governor of New Brunswick. A Biographical Sketch. Introduction by the Rev. D. D. Currie. With Artotype portrait. Clo., 12mo. 0 75

Baptisma. Exegetical and Controversial. Cloth, 12mo.... 0 75

By the Rev. D. Rogers.

Shot and Shell for the Temperance Conflict. With an Introduction by the Rev. E. H. Dewart, D D. 12mo, 184 pp. With Illustrations. Bound in handsome style, in extra English cloth, with ink stamping and gold lettering 0 55

By the Rev. E. Barrass, M.A.

Smiles and Tears; or, Sketches from Real Life. With Introduction by the Rev. W. H. Withrow, D.D. Bound in cloth, gilt edges, extra gilt 0 50

By the Rev. J. Cynddylan Jones.

Studies in Matthew. 12mo, cloth. (Canadian Copyright Edition) 1 25

"This is a remarkable volume of Sermons The style, while severly logical, reminds us in its beauty and simplicity of Ruskin. These are models of what pulpit discourses ought to be."—*Methodist Recorder.*

Studies in Acts. 12mo, cloth........................... 1 50

"No exaggeration to say that Mr. Jones is fully equal to Robertson at his best, and not seldom superior to him."—*Methodist Recorder.*

In Preparation—**Studies in Gospel of St. John.**

Books Published by William Briggs,

By the Rev. J. Jackson Wray.

Matthew Mellowdew; A Story with More Heroes than One. Illustrated. Cloth, $1.00. Extra gilt 1 25

"In Matthew Mellowdew, the advantages and happiness of leading a Christian life are urged in an earnest and affecting style."—*Irish Times.*

Paul Meggit's Delusion. Illustrated. Cloth.............. $1 00

"A strong and heartily-written tale, conveying sound moral and religious lessons in an unobjectionable form."—*Graphic.*

Nestleton Magna; A Story of Yorkshire Methodism. Illustrated. Cloth 1 00

"No one can read it without feeling better for its happy simple piety; full of vivacity, and racy of the genuine vernacular of the District."—*Watchman.*

By the Rev. W. H. Withrow, D.D.

Canadian in Europe. Being Sketches of Travel in France, Italy, Switzerland, Germany, Holland, Belgium, Great Britain, and Ireland. Illustrated. Cloth, 12mo 1 25

"Valeria," the Martyr of the Catacombs. A Tale of Early Christian Life in Rome. Illustrated. Cloth 0 75

"The subject is skillfully handled, and the lesson it conveys is noble and encouraging."—*Daily Chronicle.*

"A vivid and realistic picture of the times of the persecution of the Early Christians under Diocletian."—*Watchman.*

"The Story is fascinatingly told, and conveys a vast amount of information."—*The Witness.*

King's Messenger; or, Lawrence Temple's Probation. 12mo, cloth 0 75

"A capital story... We have seldom read a work of this kind with more interest, or one that we could recommend with greater confidence."—*Bible Christian Magazine.*

Neville Trueman, the Pioneer Preacher. A Tale of the War of 1812. 12mo, cloth. Illustrated 0 75

Methodist Worthies. Cloth, 12mo, 165 pp................. 0 60

Romance of Missions. Cloth, 12mo, 160 pp 0 60

Great Preachers. Ancient and Modern. Cloth, 12mo 0 60

Intemperance; Its Evils and their Remedies. Paper 0 15

Is Alcohol Food? Paper, 5c., per hundred.... .... 3 00

Prohibition the Duty of the Hour. Paper, 5c., per hundred . 3 00

The Bible and the Temperance Question. Paper 0 10

The Liquor Traffic. Paper 0 05

The Physiological Effects of Alcohol. Paper 0 10

Popular History of Canada. 600 pp., 8vo. Eight Steel Portraits, One Hundred Wood Cuts, and Six Coloured Maps. Sold only by Subscription 3 00

78 and 80 King St. East, Toronto.

By the Rev. J. S. Evans.

Christian Rewards; or, I. The Everlasting Rewards for Children Workers; II. The Antecedent Millennial Reward for Christian Martyrs. With notes:—1. True Christians may have Self-love but not Selfishness; 2. Evangelical Faith-works; 3. Justification by Faith does not include a Title to Everlasting Reward. 12mo, cloth 0 50

In Press—The One Mediator. Selections and Thoughts on the Propitiatory Sacrifice and Intercessions of our Great High-Priest ....

By the Rev. Egerton Ryerson, D.D., LL.D.

Loyalists of America and Their Times. 2 Vols., large 8vo, with Portrait. Cloth, $5; half morocco $7 00

Canadian Methodism; Its Epochs and Characteristics. Handsomely bound in extra cloth, with Steel Portrait of the Author. 12mo, cloth, 440 pp 1 25

The Story of My Life. Edited by Rev. Dr. Nelles, Rev. Dr. Potts, and J. George Hodgins, Esq., LL.D. With Steel Portrait and Illustrations. (Sold only by Subscription.) Cloth, $3; sheep 4 00

By the Rev. Wm. Arthur, M.A.

Life of Gideon Ouseley. Cloth 1 00
All are Living. An attempt to Prove that the Soul while Separate from the Body is Consciously Alive. Each, 3c., per hundred 2 00
Did Christ Die for All? Each, 3c.; per hundred......... 2 00
Free, Full, and Present Salvation. Each, 3c.; per hundred 2 00
Heroes. A Lecture delivered before the Y.M.C.A. in Exeter Hall, London. Each, 5c.; per hundred 3 00
Is the Bible to Lie Under a Ban in India? A Question for Christian Electors. Each, 3c.; per hundred 2 00
May we Hope for a Great Revival. Each, 3c.; per hundred. 2 00
Only Believe. Each, 3c.; per hundred 2 00
The Christian Raised to the Throne of Christ. Each, 3c.; per hundred 2 00
The Conversion of All England. Each, 3c.; per hundred.. 2 00
The Duty of Giving Away a Stated Portion of Your Income. each, 5c.; per hundred........................ 3 00
The Friend whose Years do not Fail. Each, 3c.; per hundred 2 00

Books Published by William Briggs,

By the Rev. W. M. Punshon, D.D., LL.D.

Lectures and Sermons. Printed on thick superfine paper, 378 pp., with fine Steel Portrait, and strongly bound in extra fine cloth.... .... $1 00

    This volume contains some of Dr. Punshon's grandest Lectures and Sermons, which have been listened to by tens of thousands who will remember them as brilliant productions from an acknowledged genius.

Canada and its Religious Prospects. Paper............ 0 05

Memorial Sermons. Containing a Sermon, each, by Drs. Punshon, Gervase Smith, J. W. Lindsay, and A. P. Lowrey. Paper, 25c.; cloth 0 35

Tabor; or, The Class-meeting. A Plea and an Appeal. Paper, each 5c.; per dozen 0 30

The Prodigal Son, Four Discourses on. 87 pages. Paper, cover, 25c.; cloth.. 0 35

The Pulpit and the Pew: Their Duties to each other and to God. Two Addresses. Paper cover, 10c.; cloth. 0 45

By the Rev. E. H. Dewart, D.D.

Broken Reeds; or, The Heresies of the Plymouth Brethren. New and enlarged edition................. 0 10

High Church Pretentions Disproved; or, Methodism and the Church of England. 0 10

Living Epistles; or, Christ's Witnesses in the World. 12mo, cloth, 288 pp................................. 1 00

    Rev. Dr. A. C. GEORGE, in the New York *Christian Advocate*, says:—"These are, without exception, admirable essays, clear, earnest, logical, convincing, practical, and powerful. They are full of valuable suggestions for ministers, teachers, class-leaders, and all others who desire to present and enforce important biblical truths."

    The New York *Observer* says:—"The essays are practical, earnest, and warm, such as ought to do great good, and the one on Christianity and Scepticism is very timely and well put."

Misleading Lights. A Review of Current Antinomian Theories—The Atonement and Justification, 3c.; per dozen 0 30

Songs of Life. A Collection of Original Poems. Cloth 0 75

Spurious Catholicity. A Reply to the Rev. James Roy.... 0 10

The Development of Doctrine. Lecture delivered before the Theological Union, Victoria College................. 0 20

What is Arminianism? with a Brief Sketch of Arminius. By Rev. D. D. Whedon, D.D., LL.D., with Introduction by Dr. Dewart 0 10

**Waymarks; or, Counsels and Encouragements to Penitent Seekers of Salvation, 5c.; per hundred 3 00

By the Rev. J. C. Seymour.

The Temperance Battlefield, and How to Gain the Day. Illustrated. 12mo, cloth $0 65
Voices from the Throne; or, God's Call to Faith and Obedience. Cloth.. 0 50

By the Rev. Alex. Sutherland, D.D.

A Summer in Prairie-Land. Notes of Tour through the North-West Territory. Paper, 40 cts.; cloth 0 70
Erring Through Wine..................................... 0 05

By the Rev. George H. Cornish.

Cyclopædia of Methodism in Canada. Containing Historical, Educational, and Statistical Information, dating from the beginning of the work in the several Provinces in the Dominion of Canada, with Portrait and Illustrations. Cloth, $4.50; sheep...................................... 5 00
Pastor's Record and Pocket Ritual. Russia limp, 75 cents. Roan, with flap and pocket 0 90

By the Rev. W. J. Hunter, D.D.

The Pleasure Dance and its Relation to Religion and Morality... 0 10
Popular Amusements 0 10

By John Ashworth.

Strange Tales from Humble Life. First series. 12mo, 470 pp., cloth 1 00
Strange Tales from Humble Life. Second series, cloth.... 0 45

By the Rev. H. F. Bland.

Soul-Winning. A Course of Four Lectures delivered at Victoria University 0 30
Universal Childhood Drawn to Christ. With an Appendix containing remarks on the Rev. Dr. Burwash's "Moral Condition of Childhood." Paper...... .... 0 10

Books Published by William Briggs,

By the Rev. John Carroll, D.D.

Case and His Contemporaries. A Biographical History of Methodism in Canada. 5 vols., cloth	$4 90
Father Corson; being the Life of the late Rev. Robert Corson. 12mo, cloth	0 90
"My Boy Life." Presented in a Succession of True Stories. 12mo, cloth, 300 pp	1 00
Methodist Baptism. Paper	0 10
Exposition Expounded, Defended and Supplemented. Limp cloth	0 40
School of the Prophets, Father McRorey's Class, and Squire Firstman's Kitchen Fire	0 75

By the Rev. S. G. Phillips, M.A.

The Evangelical Denominations of the Age	0 15
The need of the World. With Introduction by the Rev. S. S. Nelles, D.D., LL.D. Cloth	1 00
In Press—**The Methodist Pulpit.** A Collection of Original Sermons from Living Ministers of the United Methodist Church in Canada. Edited by the Rev. S. G. Phillips	

By the Rev. Hugh Johnston, M.A., B.D.

Toward the Sunrise. Being Sketches of Travel in the East. Illustrated. To which is added a Memorial Sketch of Rev. W. M. Punshon, LL.D., with Portrait. 460 pp., 12mo, cloth	1 25
The Practical Test of Christianity. A Sermon delivered before the Theological Union, Victoria College, 1883	0 20

Applied Logic. By the Rev. S. S. Nelles, LL.D. Cloth	$0 75
Arrows in the Heart of the King's Enemies; or Atheistic Errors of the Day Refuted, and the Doctrine of a Personal God Vindicated. By the Rev. Alexander W. McLeod, D.D. formerly editor of the *Wesleyan*, Halifax, N.S., 12mo, cloth	0 45

78 and 80 King St. East, Toronto.

Burial in Baptism. A Colloquy, in which the Claims of Ritual Baptism in Romans vi. 3, 4, Colossians ii. 12 are examined and Shown to be Visionary. By the Rev. T. L. Wilkinson. Paper, 5c.; per hundred $3 00
Catechism of Baptism. By the Rev. D. D. Currie. Cloth. 0 50
Certainties of Religion. By the Rev. J. A. Williams, D.D., F.T.L., and The Soul's Anchor. By the Rev. George McRitchie 0 20
Christian Perfection. By the Rev. J. Wesley. Paper, 10c.; cloth 0 20
Church Membership; or, The Conditions of New Testament and Methodist Church Membership Examined and Compared. By the Rev. S. Bond, Methodist Minister of the Montreal Conference. 18mo, cloth, 72 pp. 0 35
Circuit Register... 1 50
Class-Leader, The; His Work and How to Do it. By J. Atkinson, M.A. Cloth, 12mo, cheap edition 0 60

"It is practical, sprightly, devout, and full of profit. We would urge every class-leader to possess himself of a copy."—*Christian Guardian.*

Class-Meeting, The. Its Spiritual Authority and Practical Value. By the Rev. J. A. Chapman, M.A 0 10
Conversations on Baptism. By the Rev. Alexander Langford. Cloth 0 30
Companion to the Revised New Testament. By Alexander Roberts, D.D., and an American Reviser. Paper, 30c.; cloth 0 65
The Life of Alexander Duff, D.D., LL.D. By George Smith, C.J.E., LL.D., Author of "The Life of John Wilson, D.D., F.R.S.," Fellow of the Royal Geographical and Statistical Society, &c., with an Introduction by Wm. M. Taylor, D.D. Two large octavo volumes, bound in cloth, with Portraits by Jeens 3 00
Journal of the General Conference, for the years 1874, 1878, and 1882. Paper, 60c.; cloth 0 75
Journal of First United General Conference, 1883. Paper, 70c.; cloth 1 00
Lectures and Sermons. Delivered before the "Theological Union" of the University of Victoria College. 1879 to 1882 inclusive, in one volume, cloth................... 0 75
The above may be had separately, in paper covers, each.. 0 20
Librarian's Account Book 0 50
Life and Times of Anson Green, D.D. Written by himself. 12mo, cloth, with Portrait 1 00
Lone Land Lights. By the Rev. J. McLean. Cloth 0 35
Memories of James B. Morrow. By the Rev. A. W. Nicholson. Cloth 0 75

Books Published by William Briggs.

Memorials of Mr. and Mrs. Jackson. With Steel Portrait.
Cloth $0 35
Methodist Catechisms. No. 1., per dozen, 25c.; No. II., per dozen, 60c.; No III., per dozen, 75c. Three in one. Cloth. Each 0 25
Methodist Hymn-Books. In various sizes and styles of binding. Prices from 30 cents upwards.
Old Christianity against Papal Novelties. By Gideon Ouseley, Illustrated. Cloth......................... 1 00
Prayer and its Remarkable Answers. By W. W. Patton, D.D. Cloth 1 00
Recreations. A Book of Poems. By the Rev. E. A. Stafford, M.A., President of the Montreal Conference. It is beautifully printed on English paper, and bound in extra English cloth, bevelled edges, and lettered in gold 0 35
Religion of Life; or, Christ and Nicodemus. By John G. Manly. Cloth 0 50
  "Of the orthodox evangelical type, vigorous and earnest. Most great theological questions come up for more or less of notice, and Mr. Manly's remarks are always thoughtful and penetrating."—*The British Quarterly Review.*
Roll Book. Designed for the Use of Infant Classes. One-quire Book containing lines for 178 Scholars, and lasting for 13 years, $1.00; and a Two-quire Book similar to above 1 50
Secretary's Minute Book. New design. By Thomas Wallis. Boards 0 60
Secretary's Minute Book 0 50
Sermons on Christian Life. By the Rev. C. W. Hawkins. Cloth 1 00
Spiritual Struggles of a Roman Catholic. An Autobiographical Sketch. By the Rev. Louis N. Beaudry. Steel Portrait. Cloth 1 00
  "We do not remember having seen a volume better fitted than this for universal circulation among Protestants and Romanists."—*Talmage's Christian at Work.*
Sunday-School Class Book. Cloth, per dozen 0 75
Sunday-School Class Book. New design. Cloth, per doz. 1 50
Sunday-School Register 0 50
Sunday-School Record (new) for Secretaries 1 25
Theological Compend. By the Rev. Amos Binney. 32mo, cloth 0 30
The Guiding Angel. By Kate Murray. 18mo, cloth 0 30
Weekly Offering Book............................... 1 50
Within the Vail; or, Entire Sanctification. By the Rev. James Caswell 0 10

☞ *Any Book mailed post-free on receipt of price.*

www.ingramcontent.com/pod-product-compliance
Lightning Source LLC
Chambersburg PA
CBHW022111230426
43672CB00008B/1340